MW01290898

Simple Shares.....

.....Simply Said

1st Edition

Published by 5Gifts4Ever

Printed in the United States of America

3 5 2 11 21 1

Simple Shares.....
.....Simply Said

Contents

Introduction

Why am I writing this book? I am doing so because I felt a nudge to do so that wasn't going away, to share some thoughts and ideas that resonate and reverberate with me, in hopes it is of value to you. *I guarantee that when you have finished reading and get to the other side of this book you will have changed.* I don't think that is a bold statement, as I know it will be a reality. Why? The Holy Spirit will make sure you do. Basic science or psychology also proves it so for those who don't yet understand the Holy Spirit. I'm also stating you will change to set an expectation: an expectation of what you will receive; as well as an expectation that what you receive will be in direct correlation to the efforts, time and heart you dedicate.

I feel compelled to first suggest to you that it would be a shame and significant hindrance if you are arrogant, mistaken or presumptive enough to assume you are special and unique in the sins you have committed. You're not that special or creative enough in that regard, trust me; none of us are. Whether these are thoughts manufactured by your mind or have been planted by whispers of the wicked one, please come to grips now that there isn't anything you've done that is worse than me or anyone else reading this, or that you know. That is a major blocker for many. I know this from experience, as I lived it and it was a blocker for me, and I see it in others. How do I know your sins are not worse than mine or others? God tells us so. If you need worldly examples, research people who led horrific lives and went on to find freedom in Christ.

My prayers and motives are that through writing this, that whatever is contained in here may be of help to someone. Regardless of your station in life, past experiences, thoughts, doubts, or trials currently being experienced, may something or everything in here stir your heart and help make a positive impact on your tour of life here. A positive impact in one life has the repeating and resonating power to have abundant ripple effects as it spreads to others; those you know well, those you will come to know, and to perfect strangers you may encounter just once. It's not a proverbial gift that keeps on giving, it is a real gift that keeps on giving. I am sharing my thoughts and experiences, knowing some will be similar to those who read this. I have come to realize that while we each are completely and thoroughly unique individuals (thank God), we also have many commonalities in our thoughts, questions, doubts, desires, needs, actions we take and actions we avoid. This certainly applies to many you know well and not so well in your life, regardless of where they are in faith or life, whether realized or not, you and they share many commonalities.

I have one simple hope for this book and the audience it serves, and I feel very strongly this is why I was moved to write this and that it will occur. My prayer is this book makes a difference to someone, even if just for one. When my prayer is answered, and I absolutely know it will be, then this will all have been worth it.

God, please abundantly bless all who read this. Allow something in here to relate to them very specifically, or be a spark that enables them to find something and someone that does. Please bless that it brings or causes in some way for them to become closer to You; to know You in all ways; to feel and fervently believe in Your unconditional love; to accept Your forgiveness; to fully forgive others; to develop whatever knowledge, wisdom, habits, courage and character that are needed to grow in You; to love and serve others and to have a more fulfilled life. May this ignite their personal growth ultimately to the point they are the full person, the real person, that You meant them to be, and that is available to them. May they be unshackled from anything and everything that keeps them in bondage of any type, kind or degree; enjoy freedom from anxiety; and have their lives positively and permanently impacted as well as all whom they encounter. May they find true and everlasting freedom through faith.

Chapter 1

Overview

This book is intended to be light reading, as in easy to follow, and thought provoking by design and by my competency and capability levels. I am not a formally trained minster nor church leader with certificates or degrees relative to ministry. As a mere every day guy and human, I am sure some statistic or verse somewhere in here is off or could be debated or shared differently. That truly doesn't concern me, as my motive is my focus, and my motive is you.

I desire for this to be received with that understanding as I share some of what I have experienced, learned, think and believe. My hope is some of what is shared helps you with understanding an area and/or gives you some ideas to consider or reconsider. If successful, this will be manageably short in length from your time commitment in reading, easy to understand, simple to apply, and compelling enough that whomever is moved by the Holy Spirit to read it, does so in its entirety and takes action. If this connects with you well enough, action will definitely be taken on suggestions and assignments as a springboard to make real and recognized progress in your life, or someone's life whom you are helping. Whether it's the contents of this book, or thoughts or actions it generates that lead to other sources that spur real and lasting change, then this will be worthy of your investment of time and effort. Please view, and apply the results of this, as an investment *by you, in you and for you.* You matter more to God than anything else, and I hope you come to warmly embrace that if you don't already, or embrace it more fully. You matter more than you may know.

For those who are very well down the path of faith, may this generate some new beliefs or perspectives in you or further solidify those you already own. Lastly, for those who formally instruct others, whether by occupation or in response to your gift to help others discover God, I pray some of the content shines some light as to what those you serve may go through at times, so that your instruction, guidance and coaching can be most rousing and permanently exciting for them.

Regarding the content, there will not be an inordinate amount of scripture references for the reader to look up in most of the chapter content by design, which may or may not be liked by some. I am doing so as I feel the content and ideas for some readers flow more easily without continual stoppage to look up scripture passages. That is just my personal preference in reading and I am writing this in such a manner as I suspect it will be for others. Some prefer to write or read in a manner where the scripture references are quoted very frequently and in abundance on any given matter, as a topic is covered. That said, and scripture of course is beyond monumentally important, many references are included with additional suggested scripture readings in the sections on Readings and Reflection and in the sample study exercises. I am certain many formally trained faith leaders can find different, or perhaps more applicable verses. That is A-OK, for my wish is that you look up the suggested scriptures and reflect upon them after reading each chapter and discover knowledge, wisdom, and hopefully both. The scripture readings and reflection add to your retention, confidence, understanding and application of what God is telling us, for us. Mostly for convenience, the verses included are from the King James and New King James versions of the Bible, unless otherwise noted. With a couple of them, I may have used a more modern English word replacement in the reference quoted. For anyone very new to faith, there are many scriptures on most any area of life, and you are encouraged to seek additional life-giving scripture references for any and all areas in which you are struggling, or in which you have a keen interest in to learn more about to apply to your life. When you contemplate the scripture references and assignments, you will naturally find yourself seeking more, which is wonderful.

Please have a blank tablet or notebook with you while you read this to capture your notes, thoughts and ideas, some of which you may find come to you completely unrelated to an area you are reading about, which is a blessing as well. For topics and scripture verses you don't understand, honor yourself by reading more about them, and equally important, by engaging others who do understand the content well, such as a small group leader for example, and certainly your Church leadership. Also, please consider turning off your phone and any electronic devices while reading, so you can dedicate uninterrupted time to your growth.

Sprinkled in this book will be a few swings at humor, some made up words (they aren't typos), some sarcasm, a bit of trivia, and stories that I share to reinforce a point. If a story or analogy doesn't do it for you for reinforcement, create your own. Think of experiences on the topic you have that may better suit you. The first section or so are a bit slower, but provide some background to my path. Please note, whether the count of readers is 10 or 10 million, the audience experience, exposure and maturity levels will vary greatly. That said, if something is very elementary and basic to you in your path, please accept why it is included as content, as it won't be basic for others. Regarding typos, this has always been a pet peeve of mine. That said, I am sure some will be missed in the publication of this even after many edits and proofreading sessions, and I apologize in advance for that. Certain ideas or suggestions will be repeated many times over for reinforcement; they are not unintended redundancies. The content is intended to be conversational in nature; hopefully most of this will seem so to you. I've quoted sources throughout, with the exception of common phrases or where originators of a phrase or thought remain unknown. Lastly, lengthiness on any given subject is not an intended reflection on its importance. I may ramble on a bit here and there though. Hopefully, the finished product for you will be a bit unorthodox and be different in a few ways than other books written on similar topics. I'm a big fan of 'different'.

I am confident and certain a few things will absolutely happen as a result of this book. Some will have negative reactions to it. Maybe they won't feel it was worth their investment of time or don't like my style. Some who know me, have known me, or think they do, will be cynical and discouraging to or toward me (see section on naysayers). Some will spew negatives about this book or me. That is really OK; may they move forward and Godward somehow as a result of this. Some who are highly trained may take exception there aren't more 'rules' tied back to scriptural references and thoughts shared. My beliefs and faith are relationship focused, not so much rules based. Hopefully some content ruffles feathers and brings discomfort where it causes pauses in one's thinking about an area that needs addressed. Others will find this to be exactly what they needed, when they needed it and for where they are in life (which has zero to do with me as I am simply taking an action put in me by the Holy Spirit). Regardless, please keep in mind what the goal is and why I was moved to write this. If this only helps just one person, it truly has been very well worth the effort. In Matthew 18:12, Jesus asked, "What do you think? If a man has a hundred sheep, and one of them goes astray, does he not leave the ninety-nine and go to the mountains to seek the one that is straying?" I don't know, but maybe there is just one He is sending this book to that represents the one lost sheep. Time, and you, will tell. I am however entirely and forevermore grateful to have been nudged to create this as a legacy and reference item for my children, their children and their children yet to be born. A request is waiting for you at the end of the book asking for your help and feedback, which will let me know if the goals and motives of this have been successful. More on that later. I pray this may be of great help to you and where needed that you allow it to lead you to thoughts, understandings, actions, churches, people, experiences, materials and prayers that are.

Hey, thank you for reading this. I am rooting and praying for you. Be confident. Understand that in no uncertain terms – *God wants YOU, and God wants YOU to win!* He knows you can. It is a tremendous truism – reflect on that.

Chapter 2

My Struggles

Growing up, I had plenty of organized religion, and faith-based materials and schooling around me. I attended Catholic schools for half of my years in grade school, was routinely brought to church every weekend, and had Sunday school during the years I attended public schools. Growing up, my parents weren't asking for votes on whether we attended Sunday service or not, or for Sunday school. We simply went as we were told to do so. It often seemed like such a forced obligation. Some reading this had zero faith-based experiences growing up, or while they are growing up now (regardless of age, we all are still 'growing up' hopefully). Others had tremendously more. For me, I heard about, read about, was taught about, and would be tested on faith related areas, the denomination I was in, other religions, and various bible topics. I didn't always know what sunk in and what was merely my getting through or getting by whatever was on the agenda for any particular class or test. In retrospect, the reality is that it was both. Certainly, there were times, however, where I felt connected, and received gifts and development.

I viewed church completely differently then versus now, including what 'church' actually means. I felt many times what I was doing was forced, compulsory, and something I was supposed to do. Regarding faith, seldom was something smashingly captivating and exciting when I was young. At times, I would intensely be into whatever messages or teachings I was experiencing; most times I simply felt it was more like compliance and a chore. Not everything made sense, I didn't feel I grew much most of the time other than what I did at times on my own. I saw God as a strict, cranky, angry disciplinarian who would send anyone to hell that was 'bad' and I saw the bible as something to avoid as a voluntary activity, as all I saw was what I perceived to be the negatives, i.e. do this or else, people that were punished, be good or go to hell, yada, yada, yada.

So, life continued on as it does. After high school, I continued my education and began adult life. Adult life. That is a funny expression to me at times, as often we adults are immature children simply masquerading as 'adults'. In college and for years after, I stopped attending church other than when I would visit family for holidays and would join when they were going. I always had that feeling I was doing so out of a tradition of obligation. As the years went by, I became a father and returned to very consistent church attendance. I would take my children to church every Sunday, have them in Sunday school classes at certain junctures, etc. At times, I was very spiritually connected to it all; at others, I would not be, but I wanted to provide a foundation for them, especially as they were young. I was absolutely committed to that. In Proverbs 22:6 it says, "Train up a child in the way he should go, and when he is old, he will not depart from it.". Young minds are so impressionable and I always wanted faith to be a foundational part of theirs. I still do of course. I view taking children to church service and sharing thoughts on faith through the lens that if I didn't, or don't, in a big and very real sense I am making decisions and choices for them regarding faith. If I didn't or don't take them (or encourage them to attend, as mine are older now), I was or am doing them a very great harm. I'm cheating them. I'm really taking away their decision and even their very thought process in this regard. I am robbing them of so much good. As a direct result I would therefore be robbing others. That would also be creating obstacles for God. I don't think I need to create any more problems for God than I already have. I have joked in the past to myself and some close to me, that I've literally in prayer apologized to my guardian angel for all the work I have put him through! When the angels were drawing names, mine must've drawn the short straw (even when he asked for a do-over, probably many times, he got stuck with me).

Anyway, so back to being a consistent participant in church attendance. For many years, I did largely follow and repeat what I experienced when growing up in my younger days. I tend to be an avid reader, as I have always enjoyed learning. I have read tons of books over the years on a diverse variety of subjects. Regarding faith, books ranged from topics about God Himself, being saved, the denomination I was born into, people who claim they experienced Heaven or hell, forgiveness, generational curses, stigmata, visions, angels, end times, to a whole host of topics I won't bore you with listing. The books were good mostly for the moment; I'd learn something; I'd pray; I'd shortly forget about whatever the topic was and continue on with my daily, worldly life of work and being a parent (though I am sure all have added to my understandings in faith). In looking back, I don't think I always grew much as a Christian then in any one fell swoop. I did in spurts, and I believe it all was foundational to my growth over time, but I never 'stuck with it' on a consistent basis regarding my development focused to following God the way He intended I could and should for extended periods of time. There were many years, and they seemed to come in batches, that it seemed I disconnected from it all, whether spiritually, or attendance or study or all the above. I wasn't ever spiritually dead as I understand that, however I certainly had seasons of sleep and hid in hibernation from God and faith. I very seldom felt connected to spiritual growth on a long-term basis, as I would seem to just go through the motions. At times, and also not too far in the past, I stopped church attendance altogether. I always have known however, that I should be better connected with God. I always had a feeling about this, sometimes very evidently to me, other times almost not at all, depending it seemed on what was happening in my life.

I'll share some areas where I struggled, and maybe some of you can relate. I didn't want to be like 'them', whomever I imagined in my mind that I thought they were. I am referring to those who are actively and visibly living a life of prayer and belief. I always had noticed, and still do today, to me they have a different look in their eyes, an aura of true peace, love and good about them. They just simply seem visibly different, happy, kind and energetic....very good people in my mind. But for me, I didn't want to be them for a variety of really great and of course 100% accurate reasons in my mind. Listed are many examples with some thoughts following each for your review:

- In my thoughts, and am sure at times my words, I'd criticize them for being self-righteous, overreaching, and pompous.
  - *Guess what? Some are. So are we at times, or perceived to be. We are all human.*

- I'd find ways to prove to myself 'they' were hypocritical. There are and always will be stories in the media about a famous, or not so famous, church, faith-based organization, or Christian leader who falls in some aspect of life, be it in the vain lanes of theft, sexual sins, physical or mental abuses of some kind, or other ways. I'd use that to justify why I didn't want to be with those folks as somehow maybe many of them must be like that.

- o *Many have and many more will unfortunately fall, and this applies to unbelievers as well, and way more so. Regarding church leaders of whatever title or ilk, consider viewing them as Physicians as an example. Do you think your doctor or nurse never gets sick? Many joke, or not, that sometimes in a medical sense, doctors make the worst patients! But as they are human, why wouldn't we expect those in a faith teaching capacity to falter? The bible tells us we all will, and always will in some degrees. And as noted elsewhere, if I were the bad guy? I'd go full time working on their failures and falls. Don't let myopic and misplaced categorical assumptions be amongst the excuses for why you don't progress.*

- I would view 'those people' as being dorky, nerdy, people who were unable to be 'cool' so they only chose that path where they would fit in with others like them. I was 'cool' and didn't want to give that up.
    - o *You are a complete and utter dork. You are the very definition of it. You are so not cool. You are a complete nerd. I am too......to someone. I am sure there are people who have viewed me or you that way, in any era or aspects of our lives. Yep, we are very uncool to someone. Take a moment and search famous Christians if this is of help to you, regarding people whose talents or life or fame you*

may like. You'll see famous names like Mark Wahlberg, Sherri Shepherd, Tyler Perry, Carrie Underwood, Deion 'Prime Time' Sanders, and scores of others. Take a peek searching and I'm sure you will find many examples of people you view as 'cool' who are very much 'cool' being dedicated in their life with Christ. Cool in Christ.

- I thought becoming a follower would mean I had to give up all the interesting, cool and fun stuff of life. Pick your flavor of whatever that means to you (hanging out with certain friends, parties, careless and long days and nights, sleeping in, laziness, happy hours, concerts, being free to do whatever, etc.). How could I or anyone give all that up for some boring way of life I thought.
  - *What was so stunning and spectacular in the activity of my life back then, or now, that is worthy of polluting my spirit, soul and body and keeping me from God? Nothing. Take a moment and try to think of what are both positive and good things, for you and those whom you impact, that would have to be given up. Most would be incredibly hard pressed to come up with any of significance. Its fiction in our mind that we created. It's an excuse. Maybe not an intentional one, but that is what it is and is bad thought from the bad side.*

- Too much work. I felt I'd never be able to know it all so why even bother.
  - *What work? Where was/is my time being spent and on, and what that would suffer? Not much comes to mind, as there is always time for what we*

view as important. If I choose to miss a weekend service, to watch TV, or play with mobile devices, what would I be giving up? Reflect back to a random time, let's say three years ago, for every weekend you chose not to attend service. Anything super specific come to mind that was so great that prevented you from attending? Learning? Engaging others?

- Unqualified. They were better than me in that regard, they must've been at it for a very long time and knew all the answers. They must have always lived good, clean and pristine lives so they kinda just fell into it. That wasn't me though, so there was no way I could fit in with this.

  o *The Bible is chock full of tons of examples of 'unqualified' people doing God's work. So is secular life. Moses stuttered and surely felt unqualified. Check out the life of Paul before his becoming Christian. He makes Charles Manson look like a really nice kid. Jacob was a cheater, Peter is said to have had anger issues, Abraham was quite old. You can find tons of 'unqualifeds' who were called to do great things and did they do, once they responded. I am unsure who first coined the following statement, but it is proven over and over again, in the Bible, as well as every day presently, and that is 'God doesn't call the qualified, He qualifies the called!'.*

- I didn't need it. I knew there was God, I'd pray to him, and that was good enough. Who needs all the church activities, groups, bingo, study times, etc.? That is for others, I thought. It mostly was all man made for power and money anyway, I would think to myself.

> o   *If I didn't need it, why was it on my mind or your mind? Who said what I was doing was 'good enough'? Who told me that? The Bible, a true Christian, a pastor/priest/preacher? No one did. I really expected God to just give me good blessings and have me do nothing in return? Not much of a friend or relationship to be in with the One who made us; who very specifically, made you and me.*

- Not good enough. I'd think I was 'too bad' to be accepted into any church or organization that is Christian and God based, if they only knew. Surely all those who are on the right path must be way better people who never did anything like I have. They couldn't possibly have lived lives of doubt, poor behavior, had thoughts like me, took action or didn't take actions which harmed others, intentionally or unintentionally. I didn't belong.

> o   *There are lots of examples in the Bible of people who did 'more bad things' than I had. Paul as briefly noted above. He was completely dedicated and focused to persecuting Christians, through torture, imprisonment and murder. Though there is no body count listed, imagine how much more evil Paul did than you. If Paul existed today, can you imagine the news coverage that would be on him and the doubts people would cast once he converted? Yet he became one of the most influential Christians of all time once he was saved, and untold numbers have been saved and helped as a result of his efforts. He is the author of 2/3 of*

the New Testament! No one is too bad or too lost for God to turn around, IF you are willing.

- Too confusing. I'd listen to quotes, or read them, and I'd get a bad feeling and run away. I didn't want to know what the Bible said in depth on any given topic, as I was afraid of what it might say. Plus, the Bible was too confusing with the language used and it was hard to read, with the "thee, thou, believeth" etc. I saw the Bible as a great book, for what I wanted to see, but avoided anything I didn't want to see.
  - *There are many Bibles available today which are written in contemporary English and are easy to read and understand, which removes this frustration. Consider for context though, that in recent years, we have learned plenty of text phrases – how would someone from days of old view TTYL, JK, IDK, LOL or other messages like this? It's practically become its own language and we've learned it. POS? Parent over shoulder. Yes kids, I knew what POS was. Point being is we are perfectly capable of learning. There are plenty of Bibles that are easy to read and comprehend; there was back then for me as well had I looked harder.*

- What would my friends, coworkers, and people in general think of me? I wouldn't be cool as shared, and maybe they'd avoid me.
  - *Maybe it is them who are also in great need, and your changing your life, can help them as well? Do I really care if someone avoids me because I am*

doing better and helping others do better? Why would someone not in faith really care and why would I care if they did or do?

- I didn't have the time for all this stuff.
    - *There is always time for what we deem important. We make time for what choices we choose to pursue. Someone who embarks upon a new hobby as an example, where did that time come from? The reality is the time is available. We may need to reallocate wasted or unhealthy time or habits to faith, but the time is absolutely 100% available to us all.*

The list could continue on and on and perhaps you have had similar thoughts. They are common. They are not unique. You are not alone. You are more than welcome to email me and share others that you have or had. There is great power in our sharing our life experiences with others…. more on that later.

Chapter 3

Common Preventers from Growth

Many conditions, experiences, beliefs, false teachings, and habits of course can work against us in our pursuit of a faith filled life. Some of the most common ones I've encountered personally or seen in others are included for your evaluation and reflection.

Fear. Without question, fear is a powerful emotion, which can serve both bad and beneficial purposes. Fear of the unknown, often is simply being uncomfortable due to lack of experience or knowledge about something or having false beliefs about an area. We need to grapple with our own irrational fears and explode them. "Sometimes the best way to fight fear is to focus on our reason for confronting it." "Often, all it takes to conquer a fear is to change our focus." John C. Maxwell. Relative to fear or nervousness, one practice that works for me? Decide to worry later. When facing something I am to encounter that could generate nervousness or fear, I will consciously decide I will remain poised and confident, and I tell myself that I can worry about being worried about it later. It works every time in part or completely. Fear of faith commonly prevents growth, due to lack of knowledge, and false concerns.

Shame. It took me quite a while, in fact only in the recent past year to consistently and fully get over this. Shame is of satan. Remember that! It's an evil plot, designed to keep us back, to fool us into repeating mistakes, to generate thoughts of 'I am sooooo bad, God can't possibly want/love/forgive me'. It's a big one that has worked on all of us, and has existed literally since Adam and Eve. It can cause us to 'hide' from God when we have failed. A personal share of mine: I had a tendency of confessing my sins to God, and quite earnestly with all my heart, yet repetitively for those which brought up shame in me. It wasn't uncommon for me to confess a specific sin, or a general grouping of them, from decades ago, over, and over and over to God. One night while doing so, the thought that came to me was 'I must sound like a broken record to Him'. Shame is what drove that, as I felt ashamed and somehow thought I needed to keep saying sorry to God for whatever areas were involved. This lead me down a path of really studying His unconditional love for us and His forgiveness. Consider your own shame if you experience this. What has this caused for you as a result? Read in Genesis about when Adam and Eve hid in shame. Who came to find them? And once He did, notice he even made them new clothes. Shame most definitely is not from God. If you struggle with shame, please go visit with your Priest or Pastor. You really, really do need to know this one. Shame is of satan; shame is of satan; shame is of satan. Shame shackles. Once you are rightfully over this, it is life changing. Take relief in knowing shame is not of God for you to suffer.

Bad experience. Unfortunately, far too many have in fact had bad church related experiences, and some of the very worst kinds. For others, many experiences really were not bad in reality and perhaps there were various contributing factors to it. If you fall into this category, I would ask you to reflect upon how you contributed to it. With services as an example, did you attend with good intentions or because you felt obligated or forced in doing so? Did you go with an open heart truly wanting to grow with God? Maybe you were in a group or church that wasn't in alignment with you at that time? Did you attend church services routinely having a mindset of being impatient for it to be over, even before it began? Whatever it may be, please reflect on other bad experiences you have had in life and what you did about it. With many of the experiences, you discovered or intentionally found a solution. Other times, you simply avoided an area that wasn't healthy for you or didn't click with you for whatever reason. Consider this however: everyone who has dined at restaurants of any kind, invariably has had a less than desired outcome: service may have been slow, wait staff inattentive; received the wrong order; food was cold or wasn't appetizing, whatever it may have been. Did you decide to ban eating out again forever? Did you come to the conclusion that since one food establishment was bad that every single restaurant in the world is unworthy of you? If you've had a bad experience with a church, group, or person, consider how much you have missed out on and will miss out on by completely banning all people, churches, groups and pastors from your life relative to faith. Who is hurting most as a result of this? Who else is impacted by your decision? Reevaluate through a new lens. A quick note on experiences as we perceive them in our rear-view mirrors. There is the adage of 'hind sight is 20/20' and often times that is helpful. However, we often distort in our minds an event or happening, or misunderstood it due to self-limiting beliefs or incorrect information. Ask ten witnesses to an accident what happened, and you're likely to get at least five variances in stories; ask them again three weeks later and you'll most likely now have a combination of 15 accounts as to what happened. Try to be open minded in evaluating anything from the past, remove any negativity where due, but regardless, look forward.

Worthiness. To me personally, this area very much tied into shame. Tack this one on to the agenda when speaking with your pastor about shame. My not being worthy enough? I always got that part. No one is. That is one part I struggled with in human terms, in that even though God Himself said even though we are not worthy enough, we need to get over it kinda thing; as this is precisely why He sent us Jesus. I'll leave this short as your own study and pastor can shed much on this. This is a keystone belief that needs to exist in each of us (God's love for us even though we are unworthy).

Isolation. This had been my #1 self-imposed blocker that prevented me in so many ways of not just faith, but life in general. I tend to think I can handle any problem, any issue, any anything on my own. I seldom ask for help in any matter; never have. The same applied to my growing in faith for most of my years, with any volume of consistent activity. I always went it alone so to speak trying to learn and understand. Please learn from my mistake: isolation is a guaranteed recipe for big failures. It's lonely (which I never really acknowledged or recognized), its dangerous (trusting just our self to understand everything), and it is actually quite selfish (not being around others to help them and also to allow them to fulfill their purpose). It stunts our growth, it eliminates the possibility of God-intended fellowship, it is tremendously more time consuming, it opens the door for all kinds of mistakes and frustrations, and lastly, it's simply not fun! There is certainly nothing wrong with alone time to rest and recharge; in fact, it is healthy. However, I now view voluntarily chosen isolation times for extended periods of time as having the same effect as being dead to others during such times. We are hard wired to be connected with others. There is power in others. There is power in groups. Many groups exist in all walks of life, as the power of others is well known, whether it's a need for belonging, distinction, identifying, learning, feeling connected to a cause, whatever it is, and it's innately in us all, whether fully recognized or not. Marketing departments know and use this well, especially with Membership Marketing tactics. Isolation, like many things, is a habit. For those having dire or undesired consequences with this, PLEASE go talk about it with a pastor or counselor.

Doubt. satan caused the first known case of doubt in the Garden of Eden. I don't believe all doubt is caused by him, but a lot of it is and can be. Other doubts we own 100% of; and many times, we don't really know the cause. We do know doubt can crowd out positive thoughts, slow or kill progress, and delay what could be. As with most everything, doubt can serve good purposes as well. Maybe we doubt we are saving enough money for retirement to be independent of need of others, so we save more, as an example. There were many funny expressions my first college roommate would share with me. Included were such pearls of wisdom as "No clouds, no class" and "C's get degrees". Both proved to be true on many days and report cards! I digress, but another expression he shared with me was regarding taking exams, 'when in doubt, look about'. While we really should not look about as in peek at others answers when taking exams, we should look about for help and counseling with our doubts! Doubt is decimated when we recognize it, take actions, transform our view on a given matter from the lands of doubt to a firm 'without a doubt'. And for the record and for anyone wondering, my roommate referenced is a really great, witty, caring, talented and successful guy and one of my all-time favorites.

Arrogance resulting from Ignorance. Sometimes people are unintentionally arrogant due to lack of accurate knowledge. I know physicians just LOVE the patients who come in self-diagnosed about both their condition and cure; they have their own remedies and want to debate the well-trained doctor about it. This is applicable to many other fields as well when someone becomes a self-convinced and professed expert in any area, whether it is some who are buying a car, having home improvements done, discussing matters at work, or many other topics; and this certainly spills over into faith related items too. It was me many times. 'I don't need church, I pray to God directly'. 'I'll go to heaven, I know I will, because I'm a good person'. And so on. Arrogance born of ignorance, which can result from many factors and harmful influences, is a common self-induced preventer to growth and being born anew.

Commitment. Conscious commitment is clearly needed for anything of value to purposely come to fruition. Many of us have held back in developing our faith due to lack of real commitment. Commitment to change. There is an adage that says, 'change happens when the pain of staying the same is greater than the pain of change' which certainly is accurate most times. You've made a commitment already, to some degree, or you would not be reading this book, whether its because you want to help yourself, help others or both.

Some institutions, such as the military, firefighters, religious organizations and businesses use what are known as Challenge Coins to reinforce and remind their members of their commitments. They are well aware that lack of commitment greatly reduces effectiveness. Challenge Coins typically contain phrases for their commitment to some goal, fellowship, or other areas of importance. It's a reminder to them about their cause, their passion, their goal, for them and those they serve. Commitment reminders can help (see section on visuals).

I'm not sure this historical story falls under commitment for the majority of those that were involved, but it certainly did for the Captain. In the year 1519, a successful Spanish conquistador Captain Hernán Cortés, and roughly 600 Spaniards, 16 or so horses and 11 boats, made their way to Mexico to conquer the land of the Mayans. He was well aware that for over 500 years, conquerors who preceded him who had significantly more resources, failed trying to do the same. In sum, when they landed to shore, Captain Cortés didn't send his men immediately into battle. He gave some motivational speeches, as his men were not nearly as well prepared and resourced as those they were to battle. He then ordered them to set all their own ships ablaze. There would be no retreat, not even an option of one; either win or die. And they won the fight. There seems to be some debates on the facts and accuracies of all the full stories of the historical event. Regardless, many have led themselves, or others, to great or key successes through great commitment. If you aren't really committed to something, you are setting yourself up automatically for failure or a lesser level of success than you could have. If needed, create a condition that forces commitment!

Lack of true commitment, to faith or anything else, seldom does any good in a sustained fashion; in fact, weak commitment usually causes real harm.

Burn your boats….and succeed.

Habits. Habits are powerfully important, aren't they? We all have good habits, bad habits, and unrecognized habits. They are a core and bedrock component of what we are or become. They are thoughts in action. We choose our habits, and our life is a reflection of them. Physical habits are often easiest to see as the results are generally visible, be it how someone eats, drinks, grooms, exercises or whatever. Regarding our physical health, Biomechanist Katy Bowman said "none of us are out of shape. We're all in exactly the shape we've allowed ourselves to become. A sound mind is impossible without a sound body. They are not competing factions, but two aspects of one identity". It's a thought-provoking perspective which can be applied to most aspects of our life, regarding what level of shape we are in for any given area. Any area of our lives and selves will naturally grow in a direction that is reflective of how we are exercising it.

Years ago, I stopped the habit of smoking cigarettes. In that process, I learned that some who were addicted to heroin as well as cigarettes admitted they had a much easier time getting off heroin than the cigarettes. I'll skip all the discussion on the addictive ingredients intentionally added to cigarettes (over 4,000), but will share one reason people struggle with breaking that bad habit: repetition. And on a side note, if you love someone who smokes cigarettes or anyone has any unhealthy habit? Don't brow beat them. Nothing anyone ever said to me in that fashion ever helped me one iota, in fact it had the opposite effect, as it increased the negativity I tied to the process of stopping smoking (see section on my Dad's words to me on 'help'). Real and lasting change and motivation needs to come from within for most things. Anyway, let's say a cigarette smoker consumes a pack a day, which is 20 cigarettes and assume for this exercise the smoker takes 15 drags per cigarette. Calculating that out, that means 300 times per day, 9,215 times per month, or 109,500 times per year that smoker inhales a cigarette. Yes, 109,500 times per year! Wow. Hence one massively strong reason the habit is hard to break – they have conditioned their mind and body through an enormous amount of repetitions for this unhealthy activity. If you asked a smoker if they were doing any voluntary habit over 100,000 times per year, I imagine most would say no and it's not possible. If you are a smoker, maybe each drag now can be a trigger for you to say a quick prayer, as an extra 100,000 prayers each year would be good! In many cases, the person with a habit isn't even consciously aware they are doing something, be it a good or bad habit. With smoking cigarettes, once I stopped is when I realized at what times I was most likely to have smoked in the past. A few years ago, I read a really interesting book on habits, titled The Power of Habit by Charles Duhigg. It is a very interesting read on dissecting why and what we do in our lives and the power of habits. One example I've always recalled was a section on former NFL player (go Steelers), coach and commentator, Tony Dungy. As a coach, he was a very big believer in good habits and a mastermind at forming and focusing them for success. In sum, he wanted to have his players stop making so many decisions during a game and to react automatically, via well ingrained and healthy skill habits. It gave him and his players an advantage on reaction times and execution and was part and parcel to Tony becoming the first African American coach to win a Super Bowl. Coach knew and knows how vital powerful habits are.

In many customer-facing careers, particularly sales or service related, there is an expression of 'know before you go', meaning be prepared for a client meeting. Similarly, know before you go into choosing a habit what the process may be in advance, so you are prepared. With some habits, we may have disdain in the beginning and then as we progress with it, our mindset changes to acceptance, then we see positivities, and shift into another gear and mode of actually liking whatever the new habit is generating and some move into a full-blown evangelist of whatever it is and how great it is. Eventually, it becomes an unrecognized habit as it is in the fabric of us and is permanent (unless we start a new habit which undoes the positive one).

Study your habits, study habits as a topic, create new and positive habits, ultimately to the point it becomes like Coach Dungy strove for; so that they become automatic. You already have habits in place now that are supportive, as well as those that block or hinder you from becoming fully you. Evaluate them. Have a strong why, as true passion will overcome procrastination every day of the week that ends in a Y.

Unforgiveness. Everyone has been intentionally and unintentionally harmed in some manner. It will happen all our days. It's not fun and can be quite devastating. The harm done in one instance can have life altering repercussions and sometimes for generations. We need to forgive if we are to move on; not forgiving others is a really big obstacle to freedom and growth, spiritually or otherwise. Forgiving someone doesn't mean you agreed with what they did, said, or caused. It doesn't mean you need to go give them great big bear hugs, sing Kumbaya together around a campfire, or hang out. It doesn't even mean you need to see the person or even like them being near you. Some you may need to forgive could be deceased. Unforgiveness has brutal consequences and is self-induced, as forgiveness is our choice. A harm is often replayed in our minds repeatedly, often times for years. Unforgiveness rears its ugly head in our interactions with others and our choices. It can cause depression, anger, personality disorders, disbelief, devaluation of self, and ailments. Its tentacles are wide and far reaching. Paradoxically, some who don't forgive and are angry about harms they've experienced or perceive they did, in turn create pain and conflict for others by their resulting actions and choices. They hate the harm they experienced, and yet commonly process it by…. harming others. You most likely know some who lash out at others, are self-entitled, are a bully, lie often, are generally angry or negative, keep a shield up from letting others really know them, and all as a result of something they have not forgiven. Please study this in depth and discuss with a church leader, as this is one area that absolutely needs conquered in each of us, and absolutely can be!

Trust. As a noun, it is defined as a firm belief in the reliability, truth, ability, or strength of someone or something. Trust at times is innate; in most cases, trust in a given matter, person or thing is developed over time through experiences and beliefs. In developing and living faith, trust can be a prevention item for many. Do they trust in the Bible and its authenticity? Do they trust in the church congregation or denomination or teachings of it? Do they trust in the pastor and leaders? Do they trust in themselves to stick with it? Do they trust in God?

A question to ponder in secular ways. Would you trust your very life to a total and complete stranger? Would you? You already do so every single day. Some simple examples: I am sitting in my home as I write this. I never met those who built this house, I don't know any of the myriad of laborers that were needed to construct it including those who poured the foundation, put in framing, floors, electrical, gas lines, the roof, or the inspector who passed its inspection upon completion when I purchased it many years ago. Yet I trust that all of them were skilled, ethical and that my home is safe. I trust in people and a process I don't know, that my home isn't going to collapse in on me or have any other massive failures which could cause me harm or even death. You do the same in every building you enter, whether it is where you live, where you work, where you shop, or worship. We do the same with planes, trains, automobiles, etc. without giving it a thought. We trust. Every day most of us will drive or ride in transportation, on a series of roads or highways. Later this morning, I will be on a road nearby and that particular intersection has been designated as the most trafficked in my geography, with over 100,000 vehicles a day using it. I'll also be on a highway, where I will be driving around 65 MPH heading south, while opposing cars are doing similar speeds heading north; and the only thing separating us? Yellow paint. I trust other drivers will stay in their lane, adhere to the yellow painted line and not crash into me. These total strangers are trusting I won't either. This is just for perspective; very real perspective, but not often considered. For me, if I can trust in something as simple as the above, I can surely trust in what is really important and worthy. If we can trust in paint, we surely can trust in God!

In closing this chapter, please pause and highlight any of the above preventers that are yours, regardless of where you are on your journey; reflect on them quietly, try to determine the causes, seek cures and counseling, and take action. Some of these will disappear quite rapidly.

Chapter 4

Lies and Self-Deception

Self-deception can be the most dangerous of all deceptions. Why? Because it is of ourselves, and how often do we argue or debate with ourselves? It has been defined as 'the action or practice of allowing oneself to believe that a false or unvalidated feeling, idea, or situation is true.'

We are the ones who are living lies in such instances, and that is quite mighty as a formidable force in our thoughts, actions and words. Though we may be heavily influenced by many people and factors, ultimately, we own ourselves and our choices. Areas of self-deception can apply to literally any aspect of life: food, drugs, fitness, alcohol, habits, work, bosses, friends, neighbors, church, faith, finances, helping others, our abilities, our potential, our opportunities, anything.

What are a few of the reasons self-deceptions materialize?

- **Laziness/Procrastination.** Some simply form or state an opinion for sake of ease and stick with it, having never put much thought, research or experience into it, which is a big ole' form of laziness or procrastination. We've all encountered people who boldly, or out of anger, make a statement or proclamation, but when asked about it, have no substance to their position. Also, what about putting things off? 'I'll do that next year once I get x, y and z in order first'; 'I don't have time right now'; 'I probably should and I will....one day'. Exactly which day is 'one day'? It has been said that one of satan's greatest tricks is the concept of 'tomorrow', meaning we put off important things, 'I'll get to it tomorrow', expecting there will be one. For roughly 153,000 people in the world, today is their last day and there is no tomorrow. They won't get to experience 'one day'.

- **It feels good.** Deceiving ourselves on any given subject, makes it OK in our minds, as we try to block guilt or that feeling of knowing we should be doing differently. 'I know its unhealthy, but hey, so and so did WAY more of this and s/he lived to be 90'; 'I could be doing worse things, so this is my one vice'; 'who cares? You only live once, right?'; 'I like it and I'm not harming anyone'.

- **If it ain't broke don't fix it.** At times, this is chosen avoidance of a particular area of life as we develop a belief that we are fine in whatever that area may be. 'I could do better, but hey, I could do worse'; 'It doesn't *really* bother me, so I leave it alone'; 'I don't have time for that, and besides, its not really my biggest issue in life right now'.

- **Yeah but.** Consider actions such as stealing time or materials from an employer, falsely calling off sick, making excuses for missing important dates or events, not doing good things for self and others, etc.'yeah, but they make tons of money and don't pay the workers enough, and besides, they'll never know'; 'yeah, but even so and so does this'; 'yeah but just because I told a white lie doesn't mean I'm a bad person'. At best, it's a feeble attempt to minimize a consciously chosen wrongdoing.

- **Blaming Others.** 'I don't do well on tests because my teacher stinks', 'when I have gone to an exercise class the instructor bored me, so I don't go now', 'My minister's sermons do nothing for me, so why go?', 'I could have been successful if I had good parents', 'I could never get that job as my parents didn't have money for me to go to college/trade school'; 'That cop had it out for me; the guy in front of me was speeding way faster'. Prisons and rehab facilities are loaded with expert players of the blame game. So are churches, homes, governments, businesses, and all aspects of the world. Don't swim in the lake of languish - take a plunge in a pool of profit, all it takes is some mind management. (OK, maybe that phrasing was a smidge corny or a little too much). Don't follow the masses that are quick to take credit for anything in their life that is good, and even quicker to blame others, for pretty much everything that is undesired.

- **Acceptance.** Some deceive themselves into believing someone or something is a good thing, in order to be 'accepted'. Examples are endless of peer pressure which, by the way, doesn't stop when we are kids. 'I only smoke weed when I hang with him, so that's not too bad'; 'I sleep with him even though he is married, but he loves me and it's just between us'; 'everyone is doing it'; 'even she does this too, so it must be ok'. Maybe at times this happens as some are practically dying for attention of any kind, which is truly tragic, though common. Nonetheless, casting our actions on social acceptance often derives its inception from deception.

- **<u>Exposure and Focus.</u>** What are we feeding our minds? 'For as he thinks in his heart, so is he' (Proverbs 23:7). Basically, we really do become what we think about consistently. There are multitudes of books and PhD level courses on the mind and its influence on our actions and being. These range across topics, with very many focused in athletics, business and faith. Henry Ford, founder of Ford automobiles and other businesses, said "whether you think you can or can't...you are right". "Our attitudes control our lives. Attitudes are a secret power working twenty-four hours a day, for good or bad. It is of paramount importance that we know how to harness and control this great force" (Irving Berlin). There are entire books on the paramount power of our thoughts and their effect on our actions which in turn render our reality. So, what contributes to our thoughts? Naturally its what we have been exposed to, thoughts placed into us by the Holy Spirit, and thoughts influenced by evil. What are you exposing your mind to via people, media, social media, movies, news (fake and otherwise), reading, and where you spend time when not working? With technology today and Artificial Intelligence, many news stories and blogs are not even written by human beings. A very well-known newspaper posted over 800 articles over one year that weren't written by a person (and it is becoming prevalent). Imagine that – people unknowingly espousing opinions or beliefs, based on what software wrote. What we are exposed to (or expose ourselves and others to) leads to choices and actions in building even stronger ties to items of self-deception or truth.

- **ME, ME, ME Focus.** We all can be guilty of this at times and when it occurs, we need to be conscious of it and correct ourselves. Some, however, are completely absorbed in the Me Syndrome ('me first, serve me, look at me, I deserve better than thee'). I include this section for two groups: those that consistently display it with repeated and chosen personal behaviors and words; and for those that are subject to, impacted by and at times influenced to the negative in being recipients of it. 'Me-ism' is entangled with and related to a lot of behavioral cousins like rage, resentment, jealously, entitlement, narcissism, and others which come out through their words and actions. Unfortunately, every reader can most likely think of examples of people like this: a boss who mocks peers or those above him or her in rank; a parent who was largely absent that ridicules any parent they see in the press or know personally that is struggling with their duties; those that mock or criticize institutions who donate countless hours and time to help others; insulting comments about church leaders, teachers, etc. There are some who will even attack those who have voluntarily helped them in many ways many times, because they feel they were entitled to it. And besides, they must think, 'if they helped me once, they surely have more to give, right? And if they are helping others, I should be getting that, not them'. There are those who will verbally complain about a famous billionaire's charitable works saying that person should give more, yet they themselves haven't voluntarily contributed a single dollar or a single minute of their time in the past week, month, year, decade and maybe ever. Some take it to another level of just simply wanting harm to befall those they deem to have a better life than them. These are folks who many dread encountering in person or by any type of communications. Why? Because the conversation will invariably be negative and self-focused. It often contains their bragging about or looking for attention to themselves (look at me), seeking attention for something they have done. Often times the dialog will include some exaggerated suffering they encountered, because they are such a great person and without fail. Invariably they include many negative comments about others in some way, all the time, in virtually any conversation they have lasting beyond one minute.

They tend to continuously mock and belittle anyone or any institution that realistically is really just a threat to their psyche in some manner. The self-deception part with this characteristic is cataclysmic, not only to the person, but often to all around them. It is a major preventive behavior and characteristic if one is to progress with faith. It simply and quite sadly is. If you were exposed to someone like that in your formative years, and it's influenced you, really dig deep and consider why some behave this way. Put some sincere thought into it. There really are only a few reasons for most. And if it's influenced you, make a commitment to change.

Unsure if you have the Me Syndrome? For thirty days, commit you will not complain to others in written or spoken words, about other people, corporations, your job, or organizations of any kind. I am not suggesting wrongs don't occur; they certainly do; however, the Me group often times not only fabricates and exaggerates them, but looks for them. Taking a 30-day break from this at a minimum, will give the world a break. Consider taking it a step further. Using a purchase made as an example, rather than lodging a vile verbal or written diatribe about something you decide isn't perfect, send an anonymous letter (to eliminate the potential for any recompense to yourself) listing suggestions to a company that will help remedy the issue, so others can benefit. Consider the words of Sam Rayburn, "any jackass can kickdown a barn, but it takes a real carpenter to build one." We have a really great carpenter as our best example in Jesus. If you truly have positive motives to remedy a known wrong, then develop solutions. And while on this 30-day effort, check out John 8 regarding judging others. It's a really great example of forgiveness.

If this seems lengthy, it is because it is a very big pet peeve of mine. The ME habit is utterly destructive and completely counter to our developing in faith. It is a polar opposite to even simply being a nice human being. If you have it or have been influenced negatively by it and it shows up too often in your habits, begin now to figure out why and take steps to remove it, or faith development will be incredibly hard, if not impossible. Taking steps by the way may include separating yourself from friends or acquaintances who have this. Pray earnestly for those who have this and have virtually become blind to it.

- **satan.** He was the first and ultimate deceiver and he's more active today than he has ever been. Do a quick online search of satan's lies. You'll find over 8,000,000 examples at a minimum. Some have said one of his greatest lies is to convince us that he doesn't even really exist, that it is all hocus pocus or a scam the church somehow created just to scare us. Really? Can anyone show where in history that some person fabricated this crazy idea? That one day, someone, somewhere just decided to make up some fictional character, just so they could get people to come to their church? He IS evil and profusely pumps out traps and temptation through deception to us since our very beginnings. His goal is simple and well known. Reflect for a moment on Adam and Eve. Think about that – they literally spoke with God, daily, whenever they wanted. Life on earth was beyond what we could possibly imagine. And yet satan deceived Eve, who then influenced Adam, who also chose to sin, which caused consequences here on earth for as long as the earth shall exist. Adam and Eve literally spoke verbally with God and could audibly hear him whenever they liked. If they fell for his deception, how much easier of a target are we? We do have a huge advantage they did not. We are fully aware of what his gig and round-the-clock never ceasing goal is all about, which is simply to devour and destroy any man, child or woman alive today. His very first crack at doing so? Deception. Reflect on that.

This list also could go on and on. There are thousands of books and millions of articles and papers on self-deception and denial. The important part in is that we all acknowledge where we've done this, do this and probably will do so again, in some way, in the future. At times, we willfully and cooperatively deny an area as being real truth. We tend to minimize items we really know deep down are not the real truth; and we often will rationalize our behaviors or our beliefs to ourselves and anyone who will listen, to justify ourselves....to ourselves. When we do so, in many areas we really do have an effect on others, whether we realize it or not. You impact anyone and everyone you encounter, from a few second brief encounter with a stranger, to a life-long friend, family member, colleague, child, or spouse. We may not intentionally try to cause harm, but in many cases, we do. A small example – if we receive more change at the checkout counter at a store than we are due as we shop with our kids, and they see that we keep it as some self-deceived stroke of luck, what did we just teach our kids? If we have a limiting self-deceipt in any area, and we profess our justifications to others, we may be causing someone else to do the same, even though it isn't good for them. They in turn may do the same to those around them. The damages we unintentionally cause can be quite severe and lasting, often times eventually impacting people far removed from us, that we never will know. Why harm the innocent? Why harm the innocent? Why harm the innocent?

So, what does all this have to do with getting on board with faith? In the prior chapter, listed were some examples of why we delay or hesitate in pursuing and living faith. If you peek back at some of the reasons listed, and as noted many more could be for you, all fall into the categories above, as self-deception and denial. Fear falls into this as well.

It is critically important – whether for faith or simply living – that we truly spend time reflecting on the above. We've all fallen into these traps. Please take time to write down areas of your life, both generally, as well as very specifically, where you have deceived yourself. It will be of great help to you and most likely will give you some much needed and life-giving relief. Being honest with ourselves is a blessing, and it's a hard step for many.

Please take the time right now to do this. If you are not honest with yourself, its nearly impossible to have a rewarding life in any aspect. It will be impossible to be the best version of you. You won't be able to be fully you to all who you love or come to love in the future. Ask yourself the questions: why do I do this? *Really reflect on the why.* What good has come of it? What possible harm have I caused to myself? What possible harm may I have caused unintentionally to others, including people I've never met or never will? Reflect on how when we lie to ourselves, we unintentionally lie to others.

We can't move on in growing in faith without at least acknowledging the above and having it as a 'to-do' as we move forward. Otherwise, we will simply repeat the mistakes, and find ourselves only using scripture and teachings and experiences to justify what we do, say or think. Let's try to get it right. This will be very hard for some and very easy for others. But give yourself the gift of doing this exercise and hopefully apply it to your daily thinking to make positive changes and generate happiness for you. I am paraphrasing something the founding Pastor of my church said in a recent teaching which was, "Don't let your yesterdays dominate your tomorrows". This is on one of my reminder slides, one of which is included in the appendix for your review if it is of help. There are similar secular quotes, such as 'those who don't learn from history are bound to repeat it', etc. My Pastor's comments can be entire classes unto themselves, as it has many tentacles, such as forgiveness, really knowing God unconditionally loves you and many other areas. The point is to look forward.

Chapter 5

Naysayers

There will always be people who try to dissuade others from doing something different than what their opinions or comfort levels are, for their own reasons. A coworker who smokes with you on break time for years, might be greatly disappointed that you announce you are stopping the habit. They don't wish harm on you, but they may immediately, consciously or unconsciously, go into a mode of 'what about me?'. If you expect some of this with your faith, and you should, consider what people might say; process it, read scripture about it, and seek any help or suggestions needed from your Pastor or small groups or friends. Regarding your forward path to freedom and faith, some will push back with their defensive comments, such as:

'I don't need religion or faith. I'm a good person, plus God knows my heart'

> Possible thought to self: 'I wonder why they think they are a good person? Based on what? Surely they don't consider themselves to be a good person simply because they follow secular laws? I wonder if they know God's heart at all?'

'No way would I hang out with all those holy rollers. Most of them are the worst of people'

Possible thought to self: 'I don't recall this person ever even talking to me about their associating with any people of faith on a personal level. I wonder why they really say that'

'God loves everyone; I don't need some church or group acting all better than me as if they know it all''

Possible thought to self: 'God certainly does love everyone, even evil people, and unconditionally so, but relationships aren't relationships if only one is fully engaged. I wonder what they would say if I asked them how they love God back'.

'I pray sometimes. That's good enough'.

Possible thought to self: 'I wonder if they've ever considered what their world would be like if God only showed up for them sometimes? Would that be good enough?'

'I don't believe in the Bible, it's a bunch of made up stuff'.

Possible thought to self: 'I don't think s/he has ever really read any of it, much less spent time studying it. Why do they make such a strong claim about the #1 read book of all time?'.

The point is simply there will be naysayers, there always will be, and not just against faith but with any type of matter. The chroneggies (chronically negative) are out in full force and in big numbers. Media manipulation helps fuel that and there is a lot of money in misery, so industry and many institutions promote it further. You know some of the naysayers in your personal life, they are big fans of saying 'same sh&*, different day'. Pray for them in earnest. Regarding faith, consider what Rick Warren, famous author, speaker and Pastor of Saddleback Church said on this: "The thing is, naysayers aren't necessarily bad people. They may truly want what's best for you. They may love you," he said. "But they're not God. So don't treat their opinions like you would God's opinions."

Prepare yourself if you've not encountered this in the recent past. Many as said do not mean any harm to you whatsoever, their cause for being a naysayer is quite varied, and they may be unaware they are like this. If they stay in that nasty rut for a long time, they even become blind to their chronegativity. This can be an excellent opportunity in time to lead someone to faith as they see changes in you, and many will if you stick to it with your heart. It is literally amazing what God does for us and through us.

As the chroneggies come upon you, be like coral. I am not much educated in anything ocean and marine related. I do however recall a story I read many years ago which I wish I could find again. The sentiment was simply this: with some coral, the side of the coral that faces the most brutal sun exposure and constantly has waves crashing in on it becomes the most colorful and the most exceptionally beautiful. Somehow the adversity, stress and struggle are what cause the physical growth reactions that help coral create its own beauty. Let naysayers be your crashing waves to help you be exceptionally beautiful!

A note on stress. Society as a whole seems to have a common view and definition of stress. Many don't recognize that there are two types of stress: eustress (good stress) and distress (difficult stress). Think of eustress as anything that stimulates good, leaving us energized or improved in some way. The crashing waves are eustress to the coral. An athlete who needs to gain more strength? The weight-lifting they perform puts strain on the body. Intense workouts actually cause tears in the fiber and tissues in the muscles, which in turn provide growth and improvement. That is eustress. The eustress of in our lives vitalize us on to greater pastures and achievements. Try to indoctrinate this into your observations and attitudes toward the happenings in your life – the old adage applies 'that which doesn't kill us makes us stronger'. Any challenging or unforeseen circumstance may very well indeed be the eustress you need. Focus on considering such times as positives for you….and many shall be.

I feel this is a good section to add some comments on change and some who may be negative about ours. Many moons ago, I worked closely with a colleague. He was well known by all who were in any meeting with him, whether he was a participant or leading the meeting. He was and is articulate, passionate, helpful, challenging in a positive way, and always memorable. Anyway, some didn't like his message at times (naysayers). I don't know if he caught wind of this or suspected that some who used to work with him in a prior assignment made comments similar to 'He says this stuff about a, b, c but he didn't do any of that'. Anyway, I recall him sharing, and I'm paraphrasing as it has been a long time, 'There are many things I did not do in my prior roles, that I have learned through experience and others, that are very valuable and helpful to me now. If I am not growing and sharing that with others, that would be a shame'. Such a valid point and reflection. I loved it, still do, and reflect upon it from time to time. You will learn more, apply more to your life and change. Of course you will be different – in a great way, so expect the naysayers and chroneggies to snidely make comments, as if you were supposed to never change. There are many great examples of our learning lessons from others, regardless if they themselves have implemented a particular suggestion or not. Who cares if someone views that negatively? You WILL encounter naysayers, either directly or through the wonderful gossip tree, that make comments like 's/he is so full of it. It was just last week (month, year, etc.) s/he did this (said that, posted this, blah blah blah)'. I am certain some who know me, know of me, were acquainted with me at some juncture or will know me in the future will have negative, or rude things to say about me and this book, as mentioned in the overview. That is actually really, really great! It means they are aware of changes and maybe are reading this. I hope this section and others provides some type of self-reflection for my naysayers, those I know or will know, and those I don't.

My request to the naysayers – those who recognize that they are anyway - please share with me precisely when it is that you feel I, and anyone, are to make a positive change, and how you very specifically gained this knowledge. If you feel so inclined, what I would also love to learn is why is it that you are against me, someone, anyone or everyone from making positive changes for ourselves and those we impact? This really is a serious and sincere request – my contact information is in the back for those who don't know me on a personal level; all who do know me personally are welcome and encouraged to call me for this conversation.

There is no singular exact time when I, you, or anyone is to flip some magical switch and become positively and immediately much different. For some, you may have an almost instant and dramatic change in a given characteristic or habit, as that certainly happens. For me, regarding faith, it has been a many year and gradual journey. Don't let the negativity of others stop you from unlocking and unleashing the real you. The naysayers will be there…. but so will be the Yay!sayers. Some will surprise you. You'll see. Ignore the nonsense of the naysayers and be numb to their noise; or better yet, allow it to be motivation.

Celebrate your change and coming changes – and *be comfortable being uncomfortable* when you need to be! Your 'why' list, God, and others, will help you succeed!

Chapter 6

What is the Bible?

The Bible in simplest terms, is our 'how to' manual. Some describe it as an acronym: **B**asic **I**nstructions **B**efore **L**eaving **E**arth. What does the Bible say about the Bible?

"All Scripture is breathed out by God and profitable for teaching, for reproof, for correction, and for training in righteousness, that the man of God may be competent, equipped for every good work." 2 Timothy 3:16-17.

I shifted my view of the Bible over time as shared, and a lot in the past year. Previously, I only looked at parts I liked which normally was the 'good stuff', not items about judgement and wrath and areas in which it has been misused to scare or coerce people into following rules, 'or else'. A quick outline of the bible is below. This Bible is one example incidentally where people differ, as some denominations or faiths have as few as 24 books, some as many as 81; I will focus to 66 books in my outline, simply as this is common among many Christians faiths. Again, this is an overview and any and all are welcome to create their own, this is simply meant as a cursory overview for any who would like it as follows:

- It is the number one read and consulted book in the world.
- An estimated 100 million bibles are purchased each year.

- There are 66 books, 1189 chapters, 31,173 verses and over 780,000 words.
- The Bible was written by approximately 40 different men, who were inspired by The Holy Spirit, over a time period spanning over 1,500 years.
- There are two testaments, the Old Testament and The New Testament. A testament is a statement of belief. And Old doesn't mean outdated!

The Old Testament is composed of 39 books and five primary sections:

- The Pentateuch (first five books Genesis, Exodus, Leviticus, Numbers, and Deuteronomy)
- Historical books (Joshua, Judges, Ruth, 1st and 2nd Samuel, 1st and 2nd Kings, 1st and 2nd Chronicles, Ezra, Nehemiah, and Esther)
- The Poetic and Wisdom writings (Job, Psalms, Proverbs, Ecclesiastes, and Song of Solomon)
- The major prophets (Isaiah, Jeremiah, Lamentations, Ezekiel, and Daniel)
- The minor prophets (Hosea, Joel, Amos, Obadiah, Jonah, Micah, Nahum, Habakkuk, Zephaniah, Haggai, Zechariah, and Malachi)

The New Testament is composed of 27 books and five primary sections:

- The Four Gospels (Matthew, Mark, Luke and John)
- Acts (Book of Acts)
- Paul's letters to local churches (Romans, 1 and 2 Corinthians, Galatians, Ephesians, Philippians, Colossians, 1 and 2 Thessalonians)

- The Pastoral epistles (1 and 2 Timothy, Titus and Philemon)
- General epistles (Hebrews, James 1 and 2 Peter, 1, 2 and 3 John, Jude, Revelation)

Many have differing opinions on the number of books, how many sections in their mind 'officially' constitute the body of each Testament, etc.   and certainly, have many varying translations on meanings of the verses. Some have no real foundation for their opinion and simply parrot what they've heard; others come from a tremendous amount of efforts in educated study into such areas as sociology, geology, Greek/Hebrew/Aramaic languages, etymology, psychology, economics, and other fields as well. Many are right and some are wrong. I do want to share my general opinion on the variety of interpretations from this perspective: in mathematics, *division always results in less.* This applies to so many aspects of our lives. If I were satan, and thank God I am not, I'd be a big proponent of division and divisiveness. He obviously is. I'd go after really big people and areas: Teachers, Preachers, Parents, Coaches, government leaders, certainly the media and many others who influence someone intimately or in mass scale. I personally find it futile and a silly disservice to God and mankind when some engage in miniscule and argumentative intended debates that 'their' bible, or opinion, is the only correct one (or their Pastor, their church, their interpretation, etc.). It is personally irritating to me when a Christian wants to routinely argue (versus discuss) with other Christians about their thoughts on a particular interpretation of the Bible or share judgmental opinions on denominations or churches in which they have no true understanding. How about jumping off the judgment train and spending that time in a more positive manner and spread some good news and hope to those not in faith instead? Make no mistake there certainly are false teachings. My point is I don't personally get hung up on small matters of insignificance where ultimately all are saying the same thing in context. (You say tomato, I say tamotto). A secular example. A former colleague and dear friend of mine and I had the same role in the company where we worked. There was a questioning methodology used for clients and prospective clients to help identify and uncover business challenges that they may or may not be aware of, in order to determine possible solutions. He preferred one methodology with a lot of steps, I preferred another. In good spirit we would debate this often between ourselves. One day we both happened to be in the same city, and were together in a meeting with a newer sales representative providing training to the person. My colleague was excited when the meeting concluded so he could pull me aside and share how I had just taught exactly, step by step, his preferred methodology. I contended I actually had just taught the one I preferred, as it was simpler and more effective for retention. The reality? I was undoubtedly and completely 100% right and he wasn't. He knew that then and knows so now. All joking aside, the reality is the methodologies and meanings were really very much the same, drove the same outcome, but they were just packaged differently. The same is often the case with the Bible translations. Consider Matthew 7:7. Below are some different bible translations:

> "Ask and it will be given to you; seek and you will find; knock and the door   will be opened to you."
> "Keep on asking, and you will receive what you ask for. Keep on seeking, and you will find. Keep on knocking, and the   door   will   be   opened   to   you."

"Ask, and you will receive. Search, and you will find. Knock, and the door will be opened for you." "Keep asking, and it will be given to you. Keep searching, and you will find. Keep knocking, and the door will be opened to you."

The message from each, though translated slightly differently, all say what God was sharing. Don't misinterpret what I am saying; I am not minimizing that some teachings are incorrect, and there are far too many unfortunate examples of where evil intended people misquote, mistranslate or intentionally preach a false meaning to lead people down the wrong path with dire consequences. My net point on this is focus to what is important and don't get caught up in division where it is not needed; pray to God; and get involved in a true Christian congregation and hang out with those having good insight and understanding.

Regarding division, as usual, there are often times two sides to a coin. Division can be powerfully positive, as in 'divide and conquer' re: achieve more together. Focus to that side of the divide coin when you delve into division.

Go get a Bible if you don't already have one. Anyone with a phone or computer obviously has access to one via the web. Do get a physical one as well however. Unsure which one to get? Ask your church leadership or a trusted friend who's on their path. Consider going to the library and check out a few. But get one and get into it! And begin to learn verses of its teachings, on a very personal level to you. Don't know where to start? Start with the Gospel of John.

Why do many recommend we memorize verses in the Bible? I have not been great at doing this in terms of knowing hundreds of them, but is something I am working on now. There are many reasons to do so. It is a way to fill our minds with positives; it is a way to serve ourselves in areas of need; it helps us fight acting upon temptations and improve in areas of life where we need help and reinforcement; and it is a means to comfort others and to encourage non-believers to get on the right path which God intended for them.

Chuck Swindoll wrote, "I know of no other single practice in the Christian life more rewarding, practically speaking, than memorizing Scripture. No other single exercise pays greater spiritual dividends! Your prayer life will be strengthened. Your witnessing will be sharper and much more effective. Your attitudes and outlook will begin to change. Your mind will become alert and observant. Your confidence and assurance will be enhanced. Your faith will be solidified". Good stuff, huh? Jesus quoted verses from the Old Testament many times. I don't have the exact number, and there are varying opinions on how many, but the point is He did. Check out the words Jesus used when tempted by satan. Yes, He quoted verses to shoo satan away. Jesus of course is our best example of everything, so that's another really great reason to memorize some verses.

Even if one has had zero exposure to faith, you already know many Bible verses but maybe were unaware of it. Mind your own business. 1 Thessalonians 4:11; United we stand. Divided we fall. Matthew 12:25-26; A leopard cannot change his spots. Isaiah 60:1; A drop in the bucket. Isaiah 40:15; Eat, drink and be merry. Ecclesiastes 8:15; A time and place for everything. Ecclesiastes 3:1; A man after my own heart. 1 Samuel 13:14; Treat others the way you'd like to be treated. Luke 6:31; Earn something by the sweat of your brow. Genesis 3:19; Two wrongs don't make a right, but three lefts do. Ok so that one isn't from the Bible, but

I wanted to make sure you are still paying attention as you read. It is true though if you think about it.

For those who think they find memorization difficult, you've done it your whole life. Want some examples? What is your social security number? What is your address? Most know the Pledge of Allegiance. For those above a certain age, you know the components to a Big Mac sandwich from McDonalds due to a commercial with a catchy jingle years ago. You surely have memorized lyrics to some or many songs. How did you memorize all those? Repetition is a big reason, whether by compulsion or choice, as most have been repeated over and over in your life and now you know them word by word. If memorizing scriptures initially seems to daunting at all, reframe how you see this. But start. How about "Jesus wept" (John 11:35)? There, now you have one (for trivia fans, it's the shortest English verse in the Bible). How about Romans 3:23 "for ALL have sinned and fall short of the glory of God"? Now you have two. Thessalonians 5:17 'pray without ceasing". Now you are up to three. Let's go for four. How about Matthew 7:7 from above? It clearly is a verse many look to where God told us to come directly to him with our needs. A simple way for me, is that God is literally telling us to <u>ask</u> him for His help. "**A**sk and it will be given to you, **S**eek and you shall find, **K**nock and it will be opened to you". ASK! It is how I remember this verse.

Some quick suggestions? First try memorizing verses tied to your immediate needs. Review your 'why' and preventers you have had, and consider verses in areas with which you are struggling, or areas in which you simply want to know more. Know it takes time, however, while many others will resonate and immediately stick with you. Consider as part of your morning prayer ritual to choose one. Read commentary about it. Write it down. Say it out loud repetitiously. Quote it to someone the day you learn it. Text it to yourself. Write it on an index card and review on your commute to work and while on breaks at work. Once you've got it memorized, use it in part of your ongoing daily speech where appropriate. Look for aspects of daily life where the verse has, or does, reveal itself to you. Then choose another one and repeat. The goal is to help you, not for you to be able to spout off a bunch of verses in general for appearance sake. Many can quote facts and information on a lot of subjects, yet are inept in the given topic. There is a big difference in saying words, versus knowing their meaning, versus applying them! I believe God would be much more pleased with us knowing less verses and Biblical content and applying the lessons, than quoting all and living none or little of them. Don't be the always reading but never learning Christian.

Even in secular ways, it is amazing how often and deeply the body of the Bible has been studied, which is really great for all, regardless of where one is in understanding. Every single book, chapter, and probably almost all verses, have many commentaries available by those who've studied them, to help you understand them better. I'd highly recommend taking advantage of reading them. A small example for me: I misunderstood the meaning of 'fear' in the Bible for decades, and knowing what it really meant made a huge difference in my understanding and perspective. Understanding it moved my thoughts from negative and a bit afraid, to one of voluntary respect and love for God, as a gift and privilege. You will find many cases like this for yourselves; and often times an understanding you have today, may become different or deeper tomorrow, through life experience or by the power of the Holy

Spirit. As said by Dr. Wayne Dyer "If you change the way you look at things, the things you look at change". As will we.

One quick side note, as this is as good of place as any to include it. Know that much of life is hard. Plain and simple. Accept that. No one ever told us life was going to be easy, most of us just assumed it would be. Life as a Christian brings with it challenges, and the Bible tells us so. Consider reading Matthew 10:34-39 and commentaries that help explain this. Know life without faith absolutely brings many challenges and even more severely so when properly evaluated. We know life here however is finite; may your adopting the Bible and its wisdom into your life, be forevermore life changing and/or life changing to a higher degree, to the level He intended for you.

Lastly relative to this chapter, reflect upon how in the heck did the Bible actually get assembled into one book? Think about the times and the lack of technology, communications, transportation, and all modern efficiencies. It's beyond my comprehension how it all actually came together. It is an unbelievable gift of God at work then, now and forever. Just think about it from a secular and logical perspective for a moment. How did it come to be penned, spanning over 1,500 years? Beyond being a miracle that it came together, it certainly wasn't assembled for fame or fortune in secular ways by its authors. What do you think would happen today if a group scattered all over the planet, tried to put together a book with a goal to have billions believe in its authenticity and continue to read, re-read, and use it as their 'how to' instructional guide on how to live a full life as God intended, for thousands of years to come? How many other books can you think of that were first written thousands of years ago that are still read today and are completely applicable to life? How many books 'change' to the reader, as they change in their life and understanding? It's truly a one of a kind. By design.

Why do you think we have it? Why do you have it? *What will you do with it?*

Chapter 7

Is the Bible Real Today?

I felt moved to include a few thoughts regarding the relativity and application of the Bible today for your reflection. Many, and me certainly included in the past, view or viewed the Bible as some type of fictional story collection, or accounts of life that pertained to 'those times back then'; old happenings and words, not current life. All are false thoughts. The Bible is in fact a collection of stories if you will, but true ones. Because it was written so long ago, some struggle with its relevancy today; if what happened then also happens now. Though word choices and circumstances were different, predicaments, persecutions, and promises all prevail. I'll simply share just a few examples of many existing, to highlight how real items from the 'back then' era also exist today, and I encourage you to think upon many more. In no particular order:

Idolatry. What is it? Idolatry is blind or excessive devotion, or worship to something or someone, other than God. Worship can be defined as holding something in great or extravagant respect, honor, or devotion. Lots has been written about it from types (open idolatry, as in publicly visible; concealed, as in idolatry residing privately in one's heart, etc.), to various areas of life. Many get visions of large golden calves from the Old Testament, as an example, and assume stuff like this is what was exclusively meant, and it doesn't happen as much in our very own specific lives. What are some current samples of things we as a society focus to as being important to excessive and unhealthy levels? Money, status, homes, clothes, technology, physical appearances, degrees, titles, jobs, associations, famous people. The word idol is often now used lightly, without much thought to it. "S/he's my idol". Its meaning has been softened, even in a joking way. Why? To deceive us. Here are a few basic examples of idolatry happening today:

- Homes with no furniture. This happens many times where some purchase a home they can't reasonably afford because they want to be in a certain neighborhood for perceived status. Some literally can't afford to furnish the house because they overextended in such a big way on their mortgage. In similar fashion, many do the same with a car, vacation, country club membership, clothing, jewelry, or whatever. All of these items of course are quite fine and enjoyable, but not in cases when we are zealous and greedy about and for them. Using the house as an example, I don't think in most cases it is the physical structure they are after. They are focused to what they believe such things bring. They are devoting tons of time, efforts, distress and emotions chasing status in this example, or acceptance in their mind, of some sort. The items, zip code, job, or club memberships are an intended means to an end, which they'll never find in this manner. They are devoted to things in a very big and focused way, and spend more time and effort in pursuit of them than they do with God.

- Plastic. How much time do people spend on their phones? Many proudly and routinely brag about having the new model Gizmo7. What did they have to do with its design or creation? How about the 'super-duper extra platinum and I am really special, so look at me' credit card? If they dig deep, they aren't boasting about the phone, or the credit card, they are bragging about having them. Some are using them as a watered down and misplaced means to find some value in how they think others view themselves.

- Famous people/politicians/entertainers. Some get into a frenzy to have a chance to see someone famous they like. Entertainment is great, as are experiences; that said, there are unhealthy levels of many who blindly follow celebrities or the famous, to the extreme. They stand in lines for hours or even days for a chance to see them. They quote, dress, follow and publicly display their devotion to someone, in most cases that they don't and won't know, and never really evaluate why they are doing so.

I'll stop there with examples of modern idolatry as you can think of thousands more. Idolatry exists very prevalently today, and it always will when we are weak.

Raised from The Dead. Of course Jesus was, and is THE one we needed to do so for our salvation. The Bible shares many other examples of people coming back to life after dying, such as Lazarus, the son of a widow of Nain (Luke 7:11-15), Tabitha (Acts 9:36-41) and others you can find in doing a quick search.

Does this happen today? If you do an internet search on 'comes back from being dead', over 89 million results will show up. You can view results from those declared medically dead, with death ranging from minutes to days. Some of which even received coverage on national news media (shock!). Doctors often will rightfully claim God as the cause for such occurrences as there is no other medical or scientific explanation they can discover for such instances. Many expert physicians have publicly shared their experiences with such things; others have written detailed accounts of the 'impossible' happening. Some have written it off as some type of misdiagnosis or mistake, as their faith is weak. We have empirical proof of many in today's times coming back from the dead. Why struggle with believing this? Nothing is impossible for God, and this is another example of events happening today that did in eras when the Bible was written.

Martyrs. A Christian martyr is someone who is killed for their faith and belief in Jesus. Etymologically martyr has an original meaning of 'witness'. Many were killed for witnessing their beliefs in Jesus in the New Testament, such as Paul, Peter, Stephen, Timothy, and Mark. In today's world, we don't have an official count, however, its massive and uncountable. Estimates suggest over 100,000 Christians are killed each year, as a result of their witnessing to their faith. Some countries publicly have outlawed Christianity, while others have done so in practice, with the result of death, torture or both. Can you imagine what life must be like for those who have to live like this? Some have had to flee the very countries in which they were raised, because their entire families will be murdered otherwise. Think about the 'leaders' in such countries. They fear Jesus and the Bible to the point they try to kill any follower they can find. That happened in the Bible many times and in many places. Why do you think that may be? Why are these 'leaders' so fearful? What are they running from or afraid of losing?

Persecution: The early church followers were heavily persecuted, and many are now with extreme cases listed above as a few examples. What about all the subtle and not so subtle plots and schemes that happen daily? Where is faith headed toward in many civilized countries? Consider some examples in the United States: some schools ban the pledge of allegiance, due to the words, 'Under God'; lawsuits are filed to have God's name removed from currency; many have lost their jobs for praying, even when doing so privately; successful lawsuits cause the removal of the 10 commandments, certain statues, and signage from the public; active lawsuits are in play to remove the words 'so help you God' in taking an oath to tell the truth in court; a bus driver unknowingly filmed saying a private prayer for a disabled passenger was forced to resign; a military chaplain court-martialed for praying in Jesus' name; bakery owners fined a six figure penalty for refusing to make a cake for a ceremony that goes against their Christian beliefs; a long time football coach fired for saying a private prayer after a game (as he had done for years); Senior citizens that are no longer allowed to pray before meals at a senior citizens center because the meals are federally funded; and the list is sadly thousands of pages long. For those who want God removed from everything, the next time you have an insurance claim on your personal property falling under 'Acts of God' conditions, how about you don't file a claim or refund any you've received in the past? You like God then, huh?

Persecution is sick, pervasive, and it is publicly and permanently all around us, ALL THE TIME. Think this part of the Bible is relevant to today's times?

If you need to find how the Bible is relevant to today, read it more and learn so you can be cognizant. Then beware and be aware of what is happening around you, as you'll discover it is as relevant now, and for all our tomorrows, as when first assembled. It has no date of expiration, and its 'best used by' date is always the present. A couple sample questions to ponder upon:

- What policy is your local congressional representative proposing to protect the rights of Christians? Have you contacted them to learn about them?

- What are your school district's policies regarding anything faith related? What is in their history books? Is the pledge of allegiance said? What are the rules regarding the types of clothing that can be worn, Christian or otherwise?

- Abortion is the #1 leading cause of death in the USA. What is your stance on this? Have you studied the Born Alive Act bills proposed, and rejected, multiple times and made your opinions known? Do you recognize the hypocrisy of the arguments some have regarding abortion (woman's choice to abort, yet if a pregnant woman is murdered, the charge is double homicide as an example)?

- Are you comfortable wearing a shirt or jacket with your favorite team logo or brand label on it? Are you equally comfortable wearing clothing with Christian faith insignia on them? How about a bumper sticker or screen saver? Are you embarrassed to be Christian or uncomfortable saying so? If so, why?

You wanna be a radical? Be a public, proud, present, professing Christian. Fight. Fight right, but fight. Don't fail to protect God's words and will for us. Don't stay on the sidelines in fear of what others may think. We aren't meant to be meek in this regard. Silence doesn't equate to agreement in many arguments or debates, but is often assumed to be agreement. Our being silent on important matters is deafening, damaging and dumbing down society. We hear about constant political battles on various topics and how we need to care for future generations, which is true, yet how often do we hear about caring for our future children regarding faith? Wasn't that a fundamental reason many countries were founded upon?

Don't blindly follow or be silent about popular and ever-present BS that is actively promoted in society. Keeping quiet to be 'politically correct' often times is an unintended endorsement by our being invisible on matters. You ever notice what that concept even is, i.e. being 'politically correct'? It's hypocrisy in a big, bold, in-your-face and obvious way. In most cases, it is a poorly disguised reality of 'YOU can't publicly disagree with subject X, but WE can talk about it all WE want. Shhhhh!!! You be silent now as we change laws, social norms and the very fabric of society. Just stay in the shadows, go sit in the corner and shut up'. Don't shush me. It is ludicrous. Who in THE hell sold us on this trash and why did we buy into it?? I am not supposed to support and speak my beliefs, so as not to 'offend', but opposers to my beliefs can speak, tweet, march and parade all they want about virtually anything they want in any way they want in support of theirs? Let me translate if needed: 'we want free speech, so long as it's ours' is what misguided and/or evil promoters of some lunatic like ideas and laws are screaming at us. And that can be from any political bent, party or affiliation.

See anything hypocritical in this at all? Know the cumulative effects compound greatly over time, and the evidence is very tangible. Silence the voices of reason, repeatedly, and create an unrecognizable society that can't be turned back is their end game. Create rules for a miniscule minority that affect the masses against their desires and beliefs, and beat them into submission, so that such rules are not undone. The evil machine has fooled society into thinking it is bad to be good. Fear tactics are constant. Any and everything that runs counter to evil is often immediately, loudly and falsely labeled as sexist, elitist, racist, discriminatory, homophobic, xenophobic…and it is all making me claustrophobic. How about you?

Don't assume 'that could never happen here' when viewing what other countries, or people just down the street, do in seeking to destroy Christianity, and quite frankly, freedom as a whole. The signs and presence of such a tidal wave in your own country, town, and community are all around you. The devil never sleeps, and is counting on us to be asleep at the wheel most of the time. Watch the news tonight, tomorrow, and the next day. How much action is proactively being done to promote evil and destroy good? It's not at all hard to see it. My goodness, we have gotten to a point where people want the legal right to be God in ways, in proclaiming their gender, as an example, to the point weird and unimaginable categories are being created, including being genderless. It doesn't even make sense intellectually, someone identifying themselves as a consonant in the alphabet? Arrogant, misinformed, insanity? Yeah, and evilly so. People suing to have their age significantly changed on their birth certificates? People suing their parents for being born? Lawsuits are already in existence on these. What do you think will be the next areas of freedom to be attacked in a month, year or decade?

The level of compounded confusion fueled by evil, fear, ignorance, denial, apathy and laziness is mind boggling. Discrimination of any kind as an example, is absolutely horrific as we all know. The media and evil doers of society have found a way to malign innocent classes of people through false accusations of this, where they've done no such thing. Think about that. Evil people will use evil acts, in this case labeling someone discriminatory when they are not, to cause more evil. They are basically saying, 'you are not evil, but I am; you've not done an evil act but I don't care, because I am categorically accusing you of it, so that I may cause more evil, by stirring the unknowing and creating yet more division and strife'. This influence leads to many lost people being embarrassed and even apologizing for things of our very beings that only God creates. Psssst, hey guess what? I am 5'10", male, of Irish and Sicilian descent, and I was born in the United States. I will not apologize for nor be ashamed of any of that; I had zero to do with any of it. It is how He created me specifically. I don't hold others who are different than me in higher or lower regard than me; I don't think others are innately better or worse than me due to such characteristics; or more or less important or valuable than me. ALL ARE EQUAL IN GOD'S EYES AND LOVED EQUALLY (even the ones causing evil). God made me as He did, and for a purpose, and I'm really OK with that. Those who discriminate? C'mon man...at least take a shot at being creative enough to do so on something that I myself created, did or chose in myself. I have God made characteristics as I said. Whoever wants me to apologize for any of that, can kiss... my... glass, which on some days will be half-full and on others will be half-empty. You thought I was going to use a word that rhymes with glass, didn't you? It was tempting, was in my mind and yes, I will admit caused a rewrite of that sentence! I better move onto the next chapter, as I could stay on this one for hundreds of pages.

The Bible is real, its real good, and its real applicable. Do something with it. It's OK to get fired up and be visible! Check out some table tossing and chair turning in Matthew 21: 12-13. You don't need to flip tables literally, but do let the world feel your impact. Do not be a victim. Don't quietly stand on the sideline while others get bullied. Don't allow yourself to be bullied. Take a stand. Fight for yourself. Fight for yours. Be vocal and active for the innocent, the defenseless, the ignorant and the unknowing. Be a positive promoter of life.

Wanna' change the world? Change the one around you, and encourage others to do the same in theirs; it's all additive.

STAND UP FOR GOD…. He does for you.

Chapter 8

What is the church?

I want to include this for readers who are very much in their infancy in faith as 'church' is very often misinterpreted. I also will include a few points to those who are more mature in faith, but critical, at the end. The church, simply said, and as told to us, is what you are as a faithful child a God, not a building you walk into for service, or bingo, or meetings. Below is a small portion from an article on from bible-truth.org for your consideration:

'...the early translators of the English Bible improperly translated the word "ekklesia" into the English word "church" instead of "assembly" or "congregation." This translation has helped promote the false doctrine of a universal or worldwide church, a hierarchical authority over the local congregation, and the church as being a building. The purpose of this article is to show how this translation of ekklesia as "church" has adversely affected the proper understanding of the biblical doctrine of the ekklesia will demonstrate the true meaning of the word as God inspired it and reject the influence of any particular church's false theology. I appeal to true Bible believing teachers, pastors, and authors to think seriously about the church of the term "the church" and correctly use the term "Christians."

Inclusion in the real meaning of church is our being saved by Christ. We, the collective believers, by his Grace and unconditional love, become a part of Him, and by default, the church. Ceremonies and denominations don't make us the church. Rituals without regard to relationship with God are merely rituals. A common analogy used is 'going to church doesn't make you a Christian any more than standing in a garage makes you a mechanic'. Quoting scriptures don't make us part of the church. Being saved does, period. A quick note on churches you attend or may have. I was born into and participated in a major denomination virtually all my life. Since I can remember, there were some aspects I didn't agree with regarding core beliefs, teachings and requirements. This is not a condemnation of that denomination, as I am very sure many or most of its congregation find complete fulfillment in it and are utterly pleasing to God. And maybe the items I disagree with, are correct. Exploring another church type was a stumbling block for me, however, until I did. I prayed and practiced all I could at various parts of life regarding my denomination. One day, however, I finally had enough of feeling like a hypocrite – that denomination and its teachings were not going to change for me (nor should they), and I felt I shouldn't be part of its services when I had continually broken its rules and would continue to do so, as several are not my belief and I don't find scripture that proves me wrong. The change for me has been profound in my growing in and understanding God's love. I only share my own experience for anyone heavily burdened with guilt or reservations about finding God elsewhere. It's really OK, though please discuss with your current church leaders, and perhaps the ones you are considering, to ensure your decisions are in line with God's will for you. Do not leave a church without a lot of prayer and reflection, as God may have specifically placed you in that church for a reason. My changing was after decades of consistent attendance, prayer, reflection and research and I felt led to where I am now by the nudge of the Holy Spirit and I am at peace. Many are church hoppers and bounce from one to the next, and the reality is, what they bring with them is the issue in most cases, not the churches they attend. As the adage says, 'wherever I go, there am I', so make sure you're not running from something that is inside of you when making a change in a church, job, relationship, or anything. Often times our circumstances seem to repeat over and over, and we fail to see, it is us and only us that is the reason why. We all know, or will at some point, someone who never seems to find the right guy/gal, right job, right whatever. Many fail to see their patterns are most likely due to themselves, which is usually failure to deal with some type of issue, hurt, or emotion that they have experienced.

Incidentally, for anyone with apprehension about attending a physical church for the first time that they've not attended before, don't have any. If you initially are going by yourself, as I have mostly done in recent years which I will change, rest assured all will be fine. There's nothing you will do wrong or feel out of sorts with when doing so. If you are really apprehensive, simply call them and ask whatever questions you may have regarding their services.

'Going to church' as in joining a gathering of believers for service or mass or however you personally call it, is of critical importance. I think deep down we all have always really known that. We can create all the excuses and rationale we can fathom, but at the end of the proverbial day, we need to attend and do so regularly. You know that. You really do in most cases. 'I don't get anything out of church' some may say. What have you put into it? Have you ever considered your attendance is one way of showing thanks to God? It's not for our viewing entertainment, though many services are very uplifting and energetic. 'My preacher's talks are boring'. Consider writing a sermon for her/him. Give it a shot. You'll probably have new found respect for the responsibility and efforts in creating sermons, which are teachings of the very highest importance. See if you can write one that is 20-40 minutes in duration, that is factual, Biblically based, compelling, and applicable to a vast and varied audience. Your message needs to resonate with every single person, from the very youngest to the very oldest and from all walks of life, and varying degrees of maturity. I suspect 99.9% reading this won't try to write one. 'I know lots of good people who don't attend church". Excuse. There are atheists who are good people, so what is your point? 'I watch some services on TV'. That is a really great benefit we have in today's times with technology, and is wonderful for those physically unable to attend a church. For everyone else, physically attend. And let's not kid ourselves, many who 'watch on TV' don't do so regularly or without distraction. Stop sitting around collecting dust.

What is dust? Dust is fine particles, often not visible to our eyes, of something that has broken down and is all around us. Most will think of dust as dirt or messy powdery gunk that makes something unsightly or unhealthy, and can cause issues of many kinds. Think about cleaning dust off something in your home. The moment you do so, the area looks clean and you feel better; and you should. Yet, more dust immediately begins to accumulate, though you don't see it, until such time as its very visible again. The decay has been falling all round you, but you didn't notice it until it becomes unbearable enough that you clean it up. What do you think the expression 'dust yourself off' means? Church is one way to get rid of your spiritual and emotional dust. For any person living, it piles up on us daily. Going to service or mass weekly helps prevent life dust from building up to the point it is unbearable.

Your participation serves so many purposes, to you, to God and certainly others. We, as a collective society, having been heavily influenced by a truly crooked, often strange, and perverse world, really have put our Pastors/Priests/Ministers in a very precarious position. Why? Because many church leaders are afraid to strongly preach core principles, including regular attendance, as they fear losing their members, much less attracting more. What a sad reality. It is a reality though. If you attend a church of some type just on occasion, some is certainly better than none, however, doing so is probably insulting and hurtful to the church leaders. Full time Pastors, Priests, etc. have dedicated their lives to many things, daily or weekly services being a very important one. Imagine, as an example, if you hosted Sunday family dinners in your home for your friends and family. You put a great deal of time and effort into making these really wonderful. You plan and make delicious hot meals, great desserts, and create a warm ambiance for a nice, loving occasion for all to enjoy their time together and bond. Think of all the efforts in advance – planning a menu to be served, recipes to review, grocery shopping, cleaning the house, setting the table, etc. Then some of your guests show up routinely late, some show only periodically and never say when they will or won't attend so the crowd size is unpredictable, some leave abruptly in the middle of it, and some leave early toward the end every single time, disrupting the occasion and distracting others in attendance. That would be hurtful, make it difficult to plan, and would be inconsiderate. I imagine it's kinda like that for our church leaders.

Simply said, go. If you don't or won't, dig deep and figure out your why, so you change your mindset and actions.

For those more mature in faith, if needed, please do a deeper reflection in what the meaning of church is, if you routinely criticize others in their journey, beliefs and practices. It is frustrating to see, read about or hear Christians minimizing other churches and denominations. Some ridicule, or are super critical of Baptists, Catholics, Methodists, Presbyterians, Anglicans, Lutherans, Evangelicals, non-denominational churches, and so on. Often those who do are very much misinformed, and their words are unintentionally harmful, unwanted and realistically are self-serving (by trying to convince themselves of their own beliefs through attacking others). One example often lodged against Catholics and many Protestant churches and others is about statues and stain glass windows. Not that it couldn't happen, but I've yet to meet someone who worships plaster, paint and glass (much less hundreds of millions doing so all over the world in this context). "But God said we shouldn't worship idols! They shouldn't have statues or stain glass windows". You know this to be true and have witnessed this with your own eyes in all their churches or are you parroting something you once heard and didn't take the time to research? Do you realize not all of these churches even have stained glass windows as an example? Have you studied illiteracy in the middle ages? If you have not and do so, you will learn that stained-glass windows, paintings, statues and other means were a way to help make Bible stories become more vibrant and understandable to the illiterate, not as objects to worship. Perhaps stained-glass windows and the like are honoring tradition, of people who devoted their skills and efforts many centuries ago in order to help those of their brethren who couldn't read, while doing so as a means to honor God. Did God violate his own rules in Exodus 25:18-20 by giving specific instructions to place gold angels on top of the ark of the covenant? Pause on that if you are commonly criticizing other churches. The vast majority of continual critics of other Christians have no issues keeping photographs of loved ones in their home or wallets (nor should they), but don't consider that to be worshiping; they keep drawings on the refrigerator that their kids or loved ones made, yet don't see that as idolatry; they visit places like Wall Street and take photographs with the 7,100-pound famous bronze bull, but that is ok to them, as are the countless examples like all the monuments in the D.C. area and all over the world. They've not given two thoughts or criticisms about the statues of famous sports personalities outside a stadium; they've never considered the images on the very currency they spend each day; etc. Each time they have or use a $10 bill, are they not only worshiping Alexander Hamilton, but also promoting adultery since he had a famous affair? Of course not, but they choose to fight with other Christians on a lot of matters without thought or pure purpose.

To those who criticize, figure out why you do so, as it is often a product of misunderstanding and lack of knowledge. Pay more attention to words and actions, as while some may think their intention is good, they are being a pawn for division; they are often times being used by the devil to cause rife amongst Christians, and successfully so. They frequently have the same negative effect on the recipient as naysayers do, if not more. There is one way to be saved as we know, plain and simple; yet there are many varieties and flavors of how people show thanks and praise for it. Don't you think God surely loves variety? He clearly does, just look around at almost eight billion unique individuals, millions of distinct varieties of fish, mammals, grass, flowers, insects, trees; not even two snowflakes are the same. If you are commonly a critic toward other Christians, re-evaluate, cease and desist. There, now I feel much better for getting this off my chest! Sincerely, it was on my heart and I felt it was important to include.

Hopefully this clears up the true meaning of church a bit if needed, and a few reasons to consider the importance of your attendance. I felt it was important to include as the topic can be a blocker for some. Please study more and/or discuss with your pastor if more insight or help is needed.

Chapter 9

What Does 'Being Saved' Mean? How do I Get Me Some of That?

Why do you want it? Determine your whys.

Like most of this book, I am going to keep this simple, because it is. Another reason is there are many far more qualified (there's that word again) to lead you into deeper and better understanding. Actually, I take that back. It isn't complex, and I am capable, however, it is THE most important part of our entire lives, and the biggest all-encompassing gift we can receive (and share) so I highly recommend you talk with someone live, preferably in person, if you have not been saved and need guidance.

In life, when someone is saved from something, they normally are kept away from or removed from an undesired result. Someone is saved from drowning by a life guard as an example. Perhaps someone gave you a reminder that an assignment was due for school or work 'wow, you really saved me'. I believe in ways these parallel what being saved means from a Christian life perspective as well. Jesus saves us from a life of depravity and lifts us from living a life focused exclusively or too heavily on the worldly, to a life with God so good we couldn't imagine it prior to being saved by Him. And of course, it is the ONLY way for the eternity we all desire. The good news to all this? Jesus did the all the heavy lifting for us. He did the hard parts that enable us to be saved, because He loves each of us unconditionally.

What does Jesus and the Bible say to us?

"that if you confess with your mouth the Lord Jesus and believe in your heart that God has raised Him from the dead, you will be saved." Romans 10:9

"For by grace you have been saved through faith, and that not of yourselves; *it is the gift of God,* [9] not of works, lest anyone should boast." Ephesians 2:8-9

"For God so loved the world that He gave His only begotten Son, that whoever believes in Him should not perish but have everlasting life." John 3:16

This is priority #1 of all – being born again. We must believe Jesus was sent for our salvation (undeserved by us), He took on ALL our sins and sicknesses as paying for and paving our way to be in a permanent and loving relationship with God for eternity, ultimately giving a physical sign by being resurrected, literally defeating and defying death itself for us. We must repent of our sins (live life in a new way, a new direction following Him). And we must confess it – to ourselves and others. That's it.

As a free and undeserved gift, many grapple with understanding and accepting it. I struggled with this for many reasons and seasons in terms of really grasping and knowing it, and realistically, from receiving it. Many of the reasons can be found in the chapters of my struggles and the common preventers. The 'recipe' is quite easy to understand; it is not the least bit complicated. A child could recite it. That said, because something is not complex, doesn't mean it is easy. My delays in understanding and receiving this had been along the lines of 'that's it?? That's really all there is to it? Seems it should be way more complicated'. Once I realized it really is plainly explained to us in crystal clear fashion and many times over in the Bible, I was able to process it, receive it, and have great joy as a result of it, which will continue to blossom and expand.

In terms of being 'born again', and many concepts for that matter, for me and my understanding I tie things back to practicality of life examples of my own. Most describe being born again as beginning anew. I've done that in lots of ways with secular things. Take fitness as an example. I tend to go in five-year cycles it seems regarding this throughout my adult years, largely due to paying attention and discipline (ranging from decent shape, to rivaling the size and weight of a medium sized prize-winning water buffalo). Those who have not seen me in the last five years would see me looking and acting a lot different than when they last saw me, because I have literally changed. I live and choose differently relative to fitness and diet. We change, we become new in many ways, though we may not have viewed it this way in the past. Many of us have begun anew in our lives often, if you will, in such areas as graduating from school, moving out to live on our own, new careers, becoming a spouse, becoming a parent, becoming a grandparent, becoming a widow, becoming a solider, becoming a business owner, and so on. For me, reflecting like this helped me grasp being born again, beginning anew in Christ, as I had begun anew in many times in life's worldly aspects. I'll share a personal learning moment for me by considering my life, to better understand concepts and teachings; in this case, the concept of freewill. All are aware of the philosophical conversations and debates about this or have had meandering thoughts about it. How can freewill exist if God already knows what we will do? For me, being a dad made it all clear, when I pondered a hypothetical scenario as follows: when my children were young, let's say it was time for a snack. If I would have laid out raw onions and garlic on one dish, and their favorite candies on another and let them choose what they wanted, I know precisely in advance what they would pick, yet it is still their choice. It would be their freewill to choose. Just because I know what they would choose in this scenario, that doesn't diminish their freewill to choose. Make sense?

Regarding being saved, many wonderful people and churches offer a prayer, often called The Sinner's Prayer, in this regard. Mine does so every week, at every service, which is really, really spectacular and life changing. There are varying versions of this prayer that people use for this purpose, and I am sure God's hand are on all the ones based upon Him for this. I'm including two below as examples that I am borrowing (the first from Pastor and author Jimmy Evans as shared in his book "Ten Steps Toward Christ" and the second from an article from Crosswalk.com).

Lord, I have sinned and rebelled against You, a holy God. There is no excuse, and I confess my sins to You now and repent of my rebellion. I ask for Your forgiveness. I believe that You died on the cross for my sins. I receive Your forgiveness now and believe that Your blood is more powerful than my worst sins. I am now totally forgiven by You and I forgive myself. The past is behind me. I confess You now as my Lord and savior. I step down from the throne of my heart, and I pray that You will now sit on that throne as my Lord and King. Come into my heart and give me the fit of eternal life. I know I don't deserve it, but I receive it by faith as a gift of grace. I believe I am now forgiven, born again, and on my way to heaven. I will live the rest of my life for You. Fill me with Your Holy spirit, and lead me, speak to me, and give me the power to change, make right decisions and live for you. In Jesus name. Amen.

Dear God, I know that I am a sinner and there is nothing that I can do to save myself. I confess my complete helplessness to forgive my own sin or to work my way to heaven. At this moment I trust Christ alone as the One who bore my sin when He died on the cross. I believe that He did all that will ever be necessary for me to stand in your holy presence. I thank you that Christ was raised from the dead as a guarantee of my own resurrection. As best as I can, I now transfer my trust to Him. I am grateful that He has promised to receive me despite my many sins and failures. Father, I take you at your word. I thank you that I can face death now that you are my Savior. Thank you for the assurance that you will walk with me through the deep valley. Thank you for hearing this prayer. In Jesus' Name. Amen.

Most believe you are immediately saved if you have said that prayer in earnest. If you just prayed in from your heart and with faith, guess what has happened?

There is so much power and love in both of those prayers, from and through Him. They are and always will be so worthwhile to read and reflect upon again for those who are saved and for those who are considering. It is simple to understand as said above, undeserved as shared in the prayers, and all coming from an all loving and healing Jesus.

I will tell you what being saved DOES NOT require, which is giving up all your life's fun and interests in worldly matters. It doesn't mean I am giving up watching football, reading books about topics other than faith, being a fan of cars and motorcycles, practical jokes, being friends with those saved and unsaved, hanging out with people with different beliefs, etc. I only share this as some think they have to stop doing everything of interest to them in all of life. God created us to have joy; being saved gives more of that. Discuss any perceived losses of being saved with someone who is knowledgeable in this area and do self-study if this is a concern you have or have had.

When was I saved? I don't know. I really don't. I know I am, but I did not have a lightening bolt type moment. Some do, and recall the exact date, time and location, which happens, and is really great. Others, like me, are a gradual process, and I don't believe God cares, as one way isn't better than the other. My opinion is that it really doesn't matter if I recall THE date, what matters is that I had one, and that you have one. God knows when it was, and that's good enough for me, and I am sure it is for Him too. I do recall approximately when I first said a prayer similar to the above, over 20 years ago. Was that when I was 'officially saved' or was I just repeating words being spoken to me? I really don't know and I don't let the thought rent out any rooms in my mind about it; I am grateful that I am. I already believed what was in the prayer. I do know I've continued to develop, and if all goes as planned and prayed for, I will continue to do so, and gain better clarity, and deeper appreciation which I hope is a never-ending journey for me. I know I will continue to fail many times - probably even spectacularly so at times - God told us we will. That doesn't mean I or anyone suddenly becomes 'unsaved'. Though God doesn't cause sin, He will use it for good. That probably applies to general struggles as a whole. Stumbling and struggles can spark success. You ever heard of Harland Sanders? Yes, you have. Colonel Sanders. You know him from his chicken meals. He was 65 years old and penniless. Tough spot to be in for anyone, anywhere. At an age when most have long slowed down and plan to rest from work, he was flat broke. He didn't give up and fold though; instead he set out to sell his product on the road. He was told "no" 1,009 times before getting to a "yes". The rest is history. 'What does chicken have to do with being saved?!?'. I don't know exactly, but it's a great story. Maybe it is a good lesson for us all to ponder, that regardless of where we are in life and our circumstances, no matter our age, no matter what we are facing, that belief, faith, hard work and persistence pays. It is never too late, for many things, including the most important of all, being saved, until we are deceased. One thousand-and-nine times Colonel Sanders tried. He worked for it. If you aren't saved, how many times will you say you will try before you really do? If you are trying to lead someone or others to God, how many times will you try to help them?

God must like numbers, as they are so woven into life. We also like numbers, and we definitely like easy. Marketers know this, and we saps fall for many products often of questionable legitimacy: 'lose 10 pounds in 10 days'; 'learn to speak Italian in 30 days'; '7 proven ways to get very rick quickly'; '3 ways to read this book more quickly' (that was a joke). Pick a subject in marketing ads and you'll see lots of 'easy' and number of steps to success. It's a funny exercise, as many are comical as they are so outlandish. God knows however that we like our numbers and we like our easy to understand. In His love for us, He gave us both for the very most important undeserved thing for all for us, being saved. It's so simple we let our minds trick us into thinking we must've missed something. We didn't. It's clear. There is *one way and only one way to be saved. Just one*. You just read it about it above and the vast majority have heard it before many times. You see? It is very, very easy to understand. What are our choices on how to live? There are only two ways – the broad way (worldly, sin, not much thinking required), and the way with Jesus. Really simple stuff when we break it down this way, as are most subjects with better thinking, connecting with those who have better understanding, and with faithful believing.

PLEASE if you are not saved, or question whether you are, I again ask that you schedule time to talk with someone who can lovingly support you with this. Make a list of questions you have about any aspect of this in advance.

Chapter 10

Where to Start or Restart?

This will naturally vary for every person, which is a really good thing. By the way, how are you feeling so far reading through this book? Do a quick 'check-up from the neck up'. Hopefully you are feeling good, energized, optimistic and hopeful. We all have our own path. The most important part is to *take action*. Make a start. It is an amazing and well-known fact that one action leads to another which can lead to many, many more, i.e. snowball effect. You will find and realize how one thing you do opens up the door to many others, and the path seems to fall into place, maybe in ways we never imagined or could have expected, but it will. Though it certainly happens, don't expect massive lightening bolt type moments and 'bang!', that all of life completely changes in a moment's notice. However it is that your path develops and matures is perfectly OK (and our Helper, the Holy Spirit will help form and direct it). There are plenty of quite varied and colorful life testimonies, by the very famous and the completely unknown, of how they found theirs.

How about starting with a reframifcation of what today is? Our todays **ARE** the good old days to someone in the future! Consciously appreciate your future good ole' day memories of today NOW as you move along your life. It's a simple thought, harder to routinely execute, but I wanted to share if it is of help in reframing how you see your present, which is a present.

Some suggestions to consider on action items:

- **<u>Give Yourself a Break/Forgive Yourself.</u>** Whether you were born and raised with faith all around you and have simply fallen away or fallen away massively, or never knew faith at all, quit kicking yourself. We have an inborn sinful nature. All of us. Who cares where you could have been had you started earlier or committed more fully? Let all that go. Also let others go, the ones who misled you, whether due to their lack of understanding or those who intentionally have done so. Let it all go. Exhale. Let your shoulders down. Loosen up. Regarding our failures, only one, ever, lived without committing sin. Hebrews 4:15 shows us Jesus knows every temptation we do, as he lived with them when He was here in human form. Nothing you've done or failed to do is foreign to him. Nothing we've done has surprised Him. He gives us all a break, in many ways and countless times, so give yourself one and move forward. This is YOUR start or new start and YOU get to form it all.

- **<u>Don't Deluge.</u>** Don't overwhelm yourself. There are countless articles, churches, books, CD's, movies, online videos, opinions of 'do this, don't do that'. Again, do not overwhelm yourself, you deserve to treat yourself better. Often times, less is more; start where you are. You won't 'know it all' right away…. or ever. No one does. Simply start, however you start, and go from there. Deal?

- **<u>Find Your Why.</u>** Spend some time in a quiet room or place where you won't be distracted to reflect on this, whether it be your bedroom, car, local library, where ever. Invest in some alone time asking yourself why you want this. Don't cheat yourself by not spending adequate time with this or having it as a 'once and done'. It could be that life is crushing down on you in your mind; it could be a 'feeling' inside that you have lately (or for a long time) that is really nudging at you; maybe you are seeking real fulfillment; it could be the life that you have been living has caused way too much grief and pain for you or others and you need and want a new way. Maybe it's that each year fundamentally seems to be a repeat of the prior year, and enough is enough, and you want to live more deliberately. Whatever your specific reason or reasons are, write them down for yourself. I cannot emphasize enough the magnitude of importance of finding your 'why' in any important aspect of life, which is one reason I've mentioned it several times. When your 'why' is strong, your chances of success are intensified, magnified, and become magnetized which make them most probable to occur. Don't waste your time, or others, with a weak why or one meant for show as the results will seldom purposely arrive. I shared in the opening why it is I am writing this book, my motives. Of course, my children and theirs are an overriding one, as they will always have this. You are my motive too. What I did not share, as of the time I am writing this sentence, is that I also have a list of my 'why' for this book, which stands at 61 reasons at this moment, and growing. I am sure I'll add more, refine some, dig deeper into some to explore 'why the why', and will eliminate some over time. Know your 'why', it is THAT critical. Putting the nudge aside by the Holy Spirit for a moment, my long list of Why for this book I am certain has contributed to my energy to devote to it, and this has been many hundreds of hours of time to create this; and not one second has been a chore.

- **What Do You Want?** In conjunction with the above, list for yourself what it is you want from becoming more fully you and following God and living the full life He really intended for you. Some want peace and tranquility. Some want new healthy relationships. Some want to fill a void in their lives. Some want to rid themselves of guilt and self-loathing. Some want to fully walk with God, having already known or discovered to some degree why we were created. All want freedom. Some are aware of promises made in the Bible and want to rightfully claim the blessings God promised for us. This list doesn't need to be super long, but it needs to be from you to you.

- **Make a Plan.** Give thought and again, write or type down what your plan is for moving forward. My suggestion at this point would be to keep this in the short term. The plan, like any, should be specific; one that is achievable for your life circumstances; one which you will track to hold yourself accountable; and should also be realistic. There is no sense in creating a plan which isn't achievable. Why set yourself up for failure? The plan is necessary however, no matter how short or how long you choose to make it. But make it. A very overused, but 100% accurate saying, is 'if you fail to plan, then you plan to fail'. True that! Make your plan.

- **Establish Written Goals.** Tied to your written plan, write down your goals at this point. Track them. Change them as needed or as you accomplish some and create others.

Reiterating the above, keep these *written, simple, achievable* and supportive of making progress toward your Why and What you want. These can be quite simple. They must be yours specifically though with emotional attachment. One of the biggest parts as repeatedly said, is your commitment to them, as well as taking action, prayer and connecting with others. For now, all of this is between you and you and for you. Do share them when you feel comfortable with others to help you. Don't let any thoughts come into your mind as to what you think you 'should' write because you think someone else would or is what you are supposed to do. What's in your heart? Pray about them.

Items may include such things as:

- **First 30 (Or X) days:**
    - Say a prayer each morning and night beginning today
    - Buy a bible, or find one online, that is in simple modern English or whatever format resonates with you
    - Share with someone you are making a refreshed approach to life
    - Read and study a book of the bible per week
    - Visit churches you think you might like to attend
    - Ask someone for forgiveness for something you did or didn't do
    - Forgive someone, either verbally to them if possible, or in your heart
    - Research a topic in scripture on an area you are struggling (health, forgiveness, salvation,

temptation, drugs, sloth, finances, etc.). Pick one for the first month and spend real time on it, not just one article, but really spend time on just one issue a lot the first 30 days

- o Complete a self-assessment
- o You get the point…. make a plan

- **<u>Find a Church</u>.** Maybe it's a denominational one you were familiar with growing up or fell away from; maybe it's a different denomination; maybe it's a non-denominational church. You might not find the 'right' one when you first begin searching or maybe you will. Guess what? Not all churches are good ones. What is important is you find one and attend. At no time when I attended a church for the first time, be it while travelling, moving to new cities, or experiencing someone else's church they attend, have I ever felt uncomfortable. As shared previously, don't have any anxiety or angst about showing up for a service to see if this seems to be where you are being called. At the risk of stating the very obvious, look online for Christian churches in your area. If you don't have access to a smart phone or internet, do so at the library. Drive around. If you've been living where you are for any length of time, I am sure you know of some. If you are not comfortable showing up for a service, call the church as noted in a previous chapter. Ask them any questions that you have, including what their service is like. Ask if it's OK that you just show up on a given service time. You should be 100% comfortable asking if you can meet with a Pastor or member to learn about their particular church. What are their core beliefs? History? What programs/groups do they have? What resources do they have for new members? Share with them where you are in your journey. Keep an open mind and seek what you are being moved towards. Some may be too 'pushy' and insist a level of involvement right out of the gate you are not comfortable with; some may demand lots of donations; some will be 'fake' or mislead. You will figure it out and know which one is for you. And as you grow, you may find it wasn't for you after all and find another. The point isn't to routinely move from church to church, but to find one, at least for now, that you feel called to, are comfortable with, and get going. There is nothing to be afraid of – look at it as if you are a customer and are simply finding a church home that works for you. Much more could be written on this, but keep it simple and take action. And for any worried they will be the worst sinner in the church they attend? You won't be, so scratch that from your concern list if it is on it.

- **Integrate.** 'Integrated me' is one of my goals this year. What this means to me, as I become more fully me, the real me as God intended, is that I do so in an integrated fashion regarding my walks in life. I am striving to be the same me in all environments (family, friends, work, church, groups, interactions with strangers, at the gym, etc.). It was always funny to me as a young kid to see a teacher from school outside of school, say at a retail store as an example. I got to see them in normal life so to speak, outside of school, and they often seemed different. You can think of examples as well, where you only know or see a person from a particular area of life, like seeing your dentist at a movie theater as example. I want to be the same me, without having masks or uniforms to fit each avenue of life. Try to be the new you, or the new you that you are becoming in all areas of your life. It's positive reinforcement for you, is what we are meant to be, and actually, its being honest with others who need us to be us. I recognize most people struggle with this, but it's not a complex thing to do, it's simply a focus item and a habit.

- **Patience.** This is an area where I have struggled in many aspects of life! But be patient. I want to know it all and know it all right now. I realize that is not possible, for pretty much anything, much less living the life God meant for me and being the real me. The reality is I don't even know what it 'all' even is to know I want to know it all. As an example, you may not know much of anything with the Bible. It does come with time. It takes time; and time takes time. Look back on the chapter in this book on the Bible. There is a whole lot of practical guidance and writing in the Bible! And its not just the volume of words, but most importantly the proper application of them to your life. You most likely will have beliefs you had in the past that will be reframed as you learn and experience things. The journal part mentioned below is a good way to keep track of how you are growing. You have lived X amount of years thus far. There probably is not one area in life that you are 100% all knowledgeable about – no one really is. Take the English language as an example. Are you an expert at that? Can you diagram a sentence? How many pronouns are there and can you list them? What is an antecedent? Dangling participle? Are there really 150 prepositions and if so, can you name them? You get the point, there is lots and lots to know, and you will learn as you go, grow and implement Christian living in time, and in a unique way that is you! So be patient – push yourself – daily, even hourly – but be patient, as after all, it is a virtue (that I mostly lack). A funny but true comment I once read about patience: if you are patient enough, eventually grass becomes milk. Think about it.

- **Be Aware.** Take a purposeful approach to being aware of what happens around you daily. It may be simple things of how you served others without realizing prior that you have been, such as holding open a door for someone who has their hands full, giving someone that parking space close to the store, etc. Be aware of all the blessings around you. Look at the variety of life around you that maybe you haven't paid attention to in the past or took for granted; notice the good that you see every day; notice in time how your thoughts and actions are changing. Choose to consciously appreciate the good and catch yourself when you become fixated on the misery promoted by media and other sources. There is a part of our brain called the Reticular Activating System, which is considered one of the most important parts that help us with our functions of sensation and attention. Simply said, its why at times we recognize something all the sudden, and it seeks validation points for our beliefs or what we are very focused on at a given time or all the time. As an example, if I am in the market for a car, say Model ABC, I will suddenly be aware of all Model ABC's on the road around me. If I am in a room with a lot of people talking, and someone calls my name, it is why I snap to attention and focus to the person who just used my name. God hard wired us to be aware of what we pay attention to, and what you choose to pay attention to now. Focus items will seem to magically appear before you in the normal course of your day. They were always there, by the way. Be aware – be present – pay attention to life. Its pretty simple to do, but is a habit to be created.

- **Don't Compare.** Don't waste time, energy or emotion comparing where you are in your growth and understanding versus others. In the words of former President Teddy Roosevelt, "Comparison is the thief of joy." There will be people many years younger than you, the same age, or much older who seem to be way ahead of you. They probably aren't. They are just further along in their individual path. <u>God wants you, period</u>. Ever notice who Jesus hung out with and pursued? Reference Luke 5:30-32 as an example. '30But the Pharisees and the teachers of the law who belonged to their sect complained to his disciples, "Why do you eat and drink with tax collectors and sinners?" 31Jesus answered them, "It is not the healthy who need a doctor, but the sick. 32I have not come to call the righteous, but sinners to repentance." He wants you, me, and people like us, to come to him, *as we are now*. Don't compare your past to others' present and wonder if you belong. His timing is always perfect for us (though we own our responsibility to put forth our hearts and efforts). Whether this is the first time you have begun a walk toward freedom in faith, or are newly recommitted, don't compare where you are, or who've you've been, versus others or where you think you could have been. By the way, also don't compare churches, etc. with 'who cares' type items. "My church has great parking, a great choir and music, a really neat pastor, it much better than yours". Really??? This isn't to dissuade you from finding a physical church that works for you, but don't compare meaningless items. There is no such thing as one 'perfect' church in the sense of a physical building and congregation; there may be a 'perfect' church for you, however, to meet your needs where you are. If there really were a 'perfect' physical church, what would happen the moment we stepped into it? We all are so very imperfect and in so many ways, that church would no longer be 'perfect' if we joined it. Capish?

Don't compare silly things that have zero to do with you helping you. Don't compare trials and tribulations either where doing so is a negative. "S/he has it easy compared to me, no wonder s/he is doing so much better, if they had my problems, they'd be just where I am". You never really know in most cases what someone is really struggling with or going through. As my Dad wisely would share with his kids, "Don't compare disasters", meaning it's a waste of time and energy and causes self-harm when doing so to justify something that isn't really justifiable or worthy of discussion. Comparing is an often-used tactic by satan to dissuade you, yes you, from living a good life, from developing and growing faith, from having a fulfilled life.

Do compare, as in recognize, your state versus others in a light of thanksgiving. From a worldly perspective, consider your conditions of life in comparison with roughly 7,700,000,000 of our brothers and sisters around this rock called Earth. There are varying statistics, by many organizations regarding categories listed below, so I'll use 'close enough' and let you research if you like. The average per capita annual income is $3,000 (check out www.globalrichlist.com for some perspectives on your income); 1.2 billion cannot read this book (or any) as they are illiterate; roughly 850 million don't have access to clean water; as many as 1.9 billion have no access or no reliable access to electricity; and as many as 36 million will die due to starvation this year. Think about that. The vast majority of those who will read this are in very blessed surroundings versus many billions of others. Relative to starvation, maybe this can be a prayer trigger, that every single time you have a snack, pray for those without food. Next time the cable TV is on the blink, instead of getting furious, pray for those who don't have electricity. Since I was a young adult, a thought has been with me, and that is this: I am sure, the very minute I was born, if not the very exact same second, another guy was too, only I was born where I was and he was born into a ravaged, maybe even war-torn world with a continual lack of even the bare necessities, as we view them. He did nothing to be born where he was nor did I. I got the easy life versus him. Of the 7.7 billion on the planet, I would wager nearly all of them as a percentage would gladly trade their problems for mine or yours in a heartbeat. If you choose to compare your life, do so out of grateful aspects.

- **Partner with People.** Whether we like it or not, acknowledge it or not, we have a fundamental and inborn need for others. It is another characteristic and intrinsic need that is hardwired into us. Don't treat faith and your journey any differently; in fact, do as much connecting with others as you can. There will be people who have walked many similar miles as you have, as well as traveled the roads that you will, who can share their story with you, and help you. This is an incredible blessing. Make a decision to join something; some type of church group or club or ministry to help you. It would be silly not to do so. Be purposeful in deciding with whom you spend time. We often become very much like those with whom we are closest to and with whom we spend time. Reflect on: 1 Corinthians 15:33, "Do not be deceived; evil company corrupts good habits"; and Proverbs 13:20 "Walk with the wise and become wise; but the companion of fools will be destroyed (associate with fools and you will get in trouble)". This is such a known phenomenon, but we often turn a blind eye to it. Don't. Get connected with positive people.

- **<u>Serve and Help Others.</u>** Be aware when you do this and offer it to God. It's often the smallest of acts for another that absolutely makes their day. Don't think serving has to be some monumental, earth-shaking, front-page news type of event. It really, really can be the simplest of things. Try to make serving others a mindful thought and action. Mankind is at its best when we are sharing love and help with our others. This too will become a habit, and become part of who you are over time. On serving others, if you are not engaged yet with a church or not yet comfortable doing so, then consider serving someone randomly or anonymously. Simple suggestions: Write a prayer (or send a prayer card) to someone you know, do the same and mail to total strangers; when finishing a meal at a restaurant, ask the waiter/waitress for someone else's bill anonymously and/or give money towards their bill; at a toll booth give money in a cash lane to the worker and say 'this is for my friend two cars behind me'; pick up trash along a street where you live; send a caring note to someone who serves the community such as law enforcement; talk with someone who seems alone at a party or any kind of event; post free stuff online for others in need of what you no longer do; talk to a homeless person, and the possibilities are endless.

A quick share. Throughout all of writing this, many thoughts come to me continuously throughout the day which I jot down and then consider including in this, many of which I have. Yesterday around 5:30 in the morning, a thought came to me that I wanted to include something regarding this point and I added it to my list of items for this book. Several hours later right before church service was to begin, I received a text from one of my daughters whose third child was having his first birthday. I smiled when I received it, for how timely and 'coincidental' it was. Just a few hours after making a note to myself, arrived such a wonderfully nice note explaining such a loving act by a stranger. When my daughter went to pick up her son's birthday cake, the woman behind the counter told her it had been already paid for and that she should read the card that accompanied it. The card read: 'We hope you don't mind that we paid for your cake. Today would have been our daughter Name's 1st birthday, but she was born sleeping. We hope you have a wonderful birthday!'. I left out the name to protect privacy of the givers, as the name is beautiful and rare and easy to find online. Her baby's name was rare enough my daughter was able to determine whom the wonderful people were who did such a nice random act of kindness. My daughter's words: "So amazing someone could lose their child and be strong enough to make good of it". She connected with the mother on social media and thanked her, which led to their having a one-hour phone conversation and the mother shared she was having a rough morning and was happy to receive my daughter's note. She said she never shops at the grocery store where my daughter ordered the cake, but something was telling her to go inside. She shared seeing how much her act was appreciated, she is now going to make it a new annual tradition in honor of her baby girl who is in heaven. Isn't that wonderful? We never know the impact we can make on others, and this led to a wonderful conversation, and a ripple effect, as it will continue on given the conversation they had together. Amen! I am going to share one other. I am not sharing much of anything I have done or do in helping others. I feel, believe and know that I am simply a vessel any and every time I do, and sharing what you have done, beyond being told not to do so in the Bible, to me removes the intention, as it brings the attention to yourself, as if that is the motive. It really takes away from what happens. I will share a small one however, as I am indebted to this wonderful little guy. My oldest daughter is a nurse and has mostly chosen to work in a private duty capacity. One patient she cared when living a few states away from me, was a wonderful young soul, whom I never had the pleasure of meeting in person. With his mom's permission, she'd send photos from time to time and share his story. He had this spark in his eyes that would always make me smile. Tough dude indeed, as his body struggled with a rare condition, I'll leave nameless for privacy reasons. It includes a lot of very tough symptoms such as heart defects, uncontrollable seizures, developmental delays, flaccid muscles and many others requiring breathing tubes, constant monitoring and always full-time care. I believe he was in the hospital many weeks and months as much as he was at his own home. Anyway, I was very moved by him and his family, and still am. I asked my daughter to ask his mom if it would be ok if I sent him a couple toys, and I did so. Having not met him, I searched a bit, and a couple just really stood out to me amongst thousands and thousands of options that could have or did have show up in my online search. I actually just did the search again out of curiosity and over 20,000 items appear as choices. Anyway, I chose two and mailed them. After receiving them, my daughter texted me something to the effect of "Dad, there is no way you could have known this, but the toy bear? Its his favorite toy. He has the *exact same one* but its nearly broken'. What are the odds? I surely didn't pick it – something moved me to do so. It made me smile, as surely a God wink occurred. They later had a fundraiser to help offset the massive healthcare bills, which included a T-shirt, with the motto "It's not where I've been, it's where I am going". My daughter sent me one, which I keep visibly in my closet for reminders of the brave little boy and his remarkable spirit. He was called home to God at age five. He lives on I am sure in many lives, now all of yours included.   I wanted to share this regarding a wonderful family and young boy, and how we can be vessels by responding to a nudge to help or simply be nice to someone else. Serve and help – you never know what a simple act can mean, do, or cause. Though unintended, most times, if not all, when serving, helping or being kind to another, we are the true recipient of the gift we give.

- **Pay Attention to Nudges.** At times, we get a feeling or a nudge that we are supposed to do something. A few samples have been included, this book coming into existence and your choosing it to read it are among them. I want to share a very personal one for which I will be forever grateful regarding Mom. Mom had what many would consider a hard life, though she never would have. She grew up with her parents and her older brother, had presumably a pretty nice and loving childhood. At approximately age 12, her mom became quite ill and Mom took over most of a typical mother's house duties, until such time as her mom passed when my mom was 16. Shortly thereafter her father became ill, and she devoted much of her time caring for him, until such time as he passed when Mom was around twenty-one. She married Dad and they had nine children. I can't imagine the amount of work involved with all the laundry, cooking, cleaning, homework, tending to scraped knees, injuries, church, and the list goes on as all know. When the youngest of our family went off to college, Mom finally had an empty nest. Not all that long after, she suffered a massive stroke, from which she never fully recovered. Among many bodily and mental abilities, she lost most of her speech as a result, though she was able to speak out some words, including Dad's name as well as all her children, many of the grandchildren, and she would also say 'love you'. Over the course of nearly twenty years she fought various pains and challenges, some of which could not be corrected or abetted by medical knowledge or treatment, all the while being lovingly cared for by my Dad. Many times along the way she would fall, sometimes then necessitating a trip to the hospital. This one particular weekend, my younger brother was in town visiting who texted me on an early Sunday morning to let me know this happened again, and they were on the way to the hospital. I was taking my two youngest children on vacation the following morning. As this was a common enough happening, I wasn't alarmed, and thought to myself I would go visit her when I came back that Friday. I spoke with my brother later that morning; a typical type conversation when such things would occur. I went about getting my kids to church, packing and planning for vacation, etc. All day, however, it bothered me differently than normal about this fall and my conversation with my brother. It was on my mind all day. As the day went on, I kept feeling this nudge I really needed to go see her, as well as my brother and my dad, so I made the drive down to the hospital in the evening. She was still in ICU, however, was alert and her spirits were good. In the interest of brevity, I'll share we joked and laughed a bit. When I went to leave, Mom said 'love you' and I replied 'I love you too Mom" and I left. I left feeling all would be OK as it always had been in the past. As we were on vacation, her condition rapidly deteriorated more and more in many ways each day. There is so much more I could share about the happenings of this share, including a really great God wink. Anyway, three days later Mom passed to go home to our Lord. She graduated as I have always thought of it. How very blessed was I to receive a nudge to go see Mom? How perfect were our last words to each other. I am forever grateful. Pay attention to your nudges; we all get them and for a reason. Yours can be life changing for you, and others.

- **Keep a Journal.** Keeping notes helps. I take notes in services I am in at my church, group meetings I attend, items from books I read, reflections on experiences I have, and whatever it is I am being moved by, learning or want to research. In part this helps with our retention – we hear something, we write it down, in my case I then transcribe that into an ongoing document I have, and then I later read it again, usually many times over when I am looking over my notes. Repetition is the mother of learning, and many things, as the sayings go. The more I experience something, and hopefully and ultimately, then share and apply it with others, the more it becomes part of me.

Take or use anything from this chapter that works for you in starting or restarting your journey; come up with more of your own; interact with church members to get more ideas or ideas that perhaps match you better.

Chapter 11

Self-Assessment on Gifts

What are your gifts? What comes naturally? What gets you excited? It's something few take the quiet time to really consider. Many years ago, I was in a spirited debate with my father. I don't recall the specific topic but it was related to the government, the economy, etc. My dad loves a spirited debate. It took me many years to recognize he did it for the mental sparring aspect. If you said you liked subject A, he would take the opposite position, whether he believed it or not, for the enjoyment of it and for sharpening our minds (Proverbs 27:17 in action - iron sharpens iron). Anyway, in one such conversation, to support my side of the debate, I proudly with chest puffed out quoted something I recently read, which was 'we all have the equal right to make ourselves unequal'. In my mind, "bam! I got him and game over - this concludes this discussion, thanks for playing'.

I am paraphrasing, but the rest of the conversation was like this.

Dad: Is *that* right?
Me: Yep.
Dad: So you think you work hard?
Me: You know I do.
Dad: You get to work early?
Me: Again, you know I do, typically arrive at 6:30 though I don't have to be there until 8.

Dad: And you think you're being successful at what you are doing?

Me: Yeah.

Dad: So, this hard work ethic. What did you specifically do to create that?

Me: no answer – I was silent as I had no answer.

Dad: Do you really think you made that happen for yourself? You really believe you simply chose a great work ethic and created it for yourself one day? Or do you think maybe you were born with it?

That hit me like a ton of bricks. A solid right hook from Mike Tyson wouldn't have stunned me more. I unequivocally got the point. I did nothing specific to have a good work ethic – God gave me that – so I needed to recognize that and own it was due to God, not me. Furthermore, it isn't something to boast about, as I had nothing to do with that characteristic being in me. I had goals, and I am a competitive person, however, it is just how I am wired; it wasn't really a choice to create. Don't get me wrong, we need to honor our gifts and develop them. There are many sad stories we have witnessed or read about with comments like 'such a waste of God given talent. He could have been the best'; 'she could have had it all. She had so much talent, was so smart and charming, and she threw it all away', etc. We've most likely done that ourselves with talents at times, whether we realized it or not. The point is we have God given gifts built into us from our birth. And Dad taught me this, and it is a permanent blessing he gave me. I recently took some time to evaluate gifts that God gave me from birth, the ones that are inborn. The phrase that came to me for me, was 'Mattamatics' meaning what things come to me very naturally or the automatic things I do without effort or most times without even thinking. I never did this reflection in in the past, but found it to be valuable. It's a worthwhile exercise that I recommend for you. This doesn't have to be anything fancy – just a piece of paper, some quiet time and some reflection.

I was in a business meeting years ago. I don't recall what the topic was that was being discussed. The one participant had replied to a point "that's oxygen", which was apparently a phrase he used often as those based in that office clearly understood what he meant. It took a couple more times of me hearing this to understand what he was conveying. What he meant was some things are like breathing, we just do them naturally and don't give it a thought. Some or perhaps all of my or your gifts are like that too.

'Why do I want to do this reflection on my gifts?'. I believe answering this for yourself is a good exercise to help find, refine, or fully engage in what our purposes may be (more in the next chapter). There are many spiritual gift assessments one can complete which are helpful. Many are available for free on the internet, though I suspect whatever church you attend or will attend has a version. These don't take long and can be helpful in deciding what directions you should consider pursuing.

The assessments can show what areas in which you may be the most effective, most passionate about, most comfortable doing, and can shine light on our natural abilities. You will find varying lists of spiritual gifts such as:

> Prophecy – Leadership -Healing-Apostle-Service-Teaching-Exhortation-Giving-Mercy-Widsom-Knowledge-Faith-Helps-Administration-Evangelist-Pastor-Hospitatlity-Intercession-Healing-Miracles-Discerning of Spirits-Tongue-Martyrdom-Celibacy.

There are many others. All are simple to understand once you do. Examples: Mercy has been defined as a divine strength to feel empathy and care for those who are hurting in any way; Exhortation has been defined as a divine strength or ability to encourage others through written or spoken words based on biblical truth; Helps can be viewed as a divine strength or ability to work in a supportive role.

Regarding spiritual assessments, I highly recommend if you do these, do so with the guidance and coaching of a good church teacher. I am certain some would debate the use of these, the varying quality of all the ones available, and would have varied opinions on how to answer and interpret the questions and results. A great reason for seeking counseling with these is it could be easy for someone to misinterpret something, undershoot use of a spiritual gift, or misapply them. Look at Moses as an example, however. He didn't want to lead people and was embarrassed about his speech. God had other plans for him, and he does for us too, so seek coaching with this. All gifts are needed.

The physical church I attend is really wonderful and is where I believe I was called to be, at least right now, which I cover a bit more in the chapter on church. As I reflect on a typical weekend service, there are so many who dedicate their gifts, time and abilities to make this happen for all in attendance. In no particular order: someone(s) manages the parking lots (clean, safe, maintained), there are volunteers who direct members on where to park; there are always volunteers at the entrance doors welcoming attendees; there are people who staff the child care center; some staff a book and resource room; there are always some at the welcome center to answer questions for new visitors; there are people who staff a general services desk to answer any type of questions; people who prepare coffee; people who keep the facilities operating at optimum levels and maintain its cleanliness; people who make sure all the materials are in the service area; ushers to direct anyone needing help in finding a seat; people who help collect tithes; many who share their gifts of voice and music who lead this portion of the service; many share their skills with audio and visual equipment; those who speak to the congregation on church happenings, resources and services; the Pastors who share words of wisdom during the service, and the list could go on further. That's a whole lot of people! That's also a whole lot of varying skills. Remove any of them, and the outcome is less, and certainly less than it could be. Every contributor makes the service happen and their absence would be noticed and felt. The same applies to all of us in life, whether in the home, workplace, church, or community as a whole. We all have very important parts to play.

We all are a God made and hand-chosen piece to the puzzle, without whom, a less than possible outcome occurs. Take some time to evaluate your gifts, for they are great, and are greatly needed. Your unique way of acting upon them makes them very especially yours. You will leave absolutely leave your imprint on life, do so positively with your gifts.

Chapter 12

Purpose

What is your purpose? Why are you here? Ah, the ever-present question since the beginning of time that mankind has pondered. Simply said, purpose is why God made us and with what he gave to us; it is what we are to do and where we are to fit, and it helps define which lane in life is ours to occupy and use to glorify God and enjoy Him forever.

My suggestion, to borrow a former colleague's expression, is don't overcomplexify it. One can spend hours upon hours searching in an attempt to find 'the one' reason they think they were made. That is definitely a worthwhile activity to explore, but not when it will drive you nuts. For me and I suspect all, there is not just one purpose, there are many. We all have roles to fill, just like every single part of our body, parts of a car, components of a computer, or a member of a family each serve a purpose. The whole doesn't work as it should or could, or at times work at all, when one item or person is absent or misfiring.

In the last chapter, we reviewed developing your list of 'youamatics' and a gifts assessment. Those can be great starting points for anyone unsure of what purposes they believe they were made to fulfill. A couple condensed examples of purposes for: Martin Luther King – unite people and promote equality; Nelson Mandela – support what respects people and enhances freedom. Purposes are individual. One may be called to teach others, build homes, heal people through medicine, counseling or friendship, create wonderful businesses and provide jobs, work for beautifying and preserving nature, actively leading others to God, administrative work keeping a family/company/church/community organized and efficient, etc. Paul said it much better in Romans 12: 6-8 "We have different gifts, according to the grace given us. If a man's gift is prophesying, let him use it in proportion to his faith. If it is serving, let him serve; if it is teaching, let him teach; if it is encouraging, let him encourage; if it is leadership, let him govern diligently; if it is showing mercy, let him do it cheerfully."

Research, reflect and speak with your pastor or group leaders, mentor, or friends and try to determine yours. I know what mine are at the moment or at least I think I do. I also know I will discover others and/or refine how I view them. I suspect there is much more to be revealed to me and I consider it a blessed work in progress which will be ongoing. Surely there will be times where God has other purposes for me that at the moment haven't even crossed my mind or life yet, or ones that are present that I don't yet understand.

A couple quick notes for your consideration. I'm not aware of any evidence that God changes his mind, and my belief is He doesn't. Some scripture may seem he does when holds back something or gives a chance for something to work out, however, His ways are not ours, and we don't understand it all. Many have said once we are called, or finally recognize we have been, that calling never goes away. The Bible tells us so as well in Romans 11:29, "For the gifts and the calling of God are irrevocable." That's an immeasurably good thing. We may try to ignore it, or go in and out of pursuing it, as I did many seasons, but the calling remains. That nudge? That desire you have? Its never leaving. And regarding gifts, if something is a gift, why would God take it back?

A life lesson and perspective, however, I learned from my Dad, who learned from his Dad. I really do know that helping others is one of my callings as its inborn. Sometimes begrudgingly. Anyway, many years ago, I was helping Dad clean out our garage. I don't recall specifically what I was doing, but was rearranging or doing general cleaning. Dad stopped me from whatever it was, as it wasn't what he needed or wanted, or was causing the garage to be worse off. I responded a bit flustered with "Dad! I was just trying to help!". I recall Dad pausing and smiling and saying, "let me share with you something my father shared with me: help is defined by the one who receives it, not by the one who gives it". That was a teaching moment and obviously one of impact that I have not only always remembered and have tried to apply, but have shared with many, including you as of now. How does this tie into purpose? Be mindful of others' needs. Where we think we may be 'helping' we may unintentionally be doing the opposite. I mentioned cigarette smoking earlier in this book, referencing this part. Don't assume you know what someone else needs. Telling someone whose heavily addicted to drugs 'you just need to stop!'; someone in a deep depression 'you need to smile more and get out of your funk!'; someone struggling with weight 'you should eat healthier', while well intended, are most likely not of help to them whatsoever and leave the person worse off before the encounter. Helping others is certainly a great purpose; misapplying it can have the opposite result. We need to ask at times and not assume what 'help' is to someone with their specific needs. Regarding our gifts, we also need to keep an open heart and mind on corrections provided to us, as they so often help us to further develop. Be cognizant of your natural gifts and skills as well as those you will develop. There are many things I would like to do, that I am naturally horrible at doing. Want me to build your kids a tree house? You really don't unless you have some weird desire to see a tree and your kids maimed in some way when the tree house collapses. Your car having mechanical issues? Cut me loose on it and it will have many more issues when I am done. I have a cousin, Mary, who is wonderfully gifted with a beautiful singing voice. She has shared her gift often at many events, funerals, weddings, and joyful celebrations. She likes to sing. I like to sing. She sings great. I don't. Years ago, she sang the National Anthem for a Major League Baseball game. Imagine if in some weird cosmic event I got put in her place at the last second. The only group of people who would have been happy about it would have been the beer vendors as their sales would have skyrocketed. The adults would have been chugging them as fast as they could to dull and dampen the audible torture they were enduring while others would be whipping full cans of beer at me to get me off the field! I am sure the sports highlights reel would have been a joy to watch, especially as the camera zooms in on the field maintenance workers caught on film tossing full cans back to the crowd so they could take another shot at me. Not all that we wish we could do will come to fruition, as its not in our gift wheelhouse: many things are someone else's lane to fill.

In my work over the years, and common to many organizations in reviewing personnel, is assessing someone's skill/will or can do/will do. Does the person have the skill? Do they have the will to learn it, develop it and apply it? This applies here as well. Some skills are within us that have been lying dormant, and need developed. Don't make the faulty assumption with some that because you don't know something or are not proficient in it right now that it isn't something you can do or were meant to do quite fabulously. We also may have blind spots. There is something known as the Dunning-Kruger effect, which is basically when someone believes that they are smarter and more capable in a given skill than the reality, and they don't recognize it. May we all have someone in life who loves us enough to tell us this when we are blind!

Do your assessment, take private time to reflect on what comes naturally, think about which areas you are passionate about, and ask others for their insights who know you. This is a great way to begin. For me, I am sure this is like the 'peel back the onion' analogy often used. I am sure there are skills we all have with more resident layers than we knew, as well as other skills we've yet to discover.

You were made on purpose, for a purpose. Maybe your purpose is to help others fulfill theirs? Maybe you have many? Discover them and make the come uniquely alive through you.

Chapter 13

Reinforcement Suggestions

Like with anything new, or newly committed to, helpful reminders and reinforcements are supportive to our success. Assuming the items listed in prior chapters have been completed with a true focus and reflection, included in this chapter are some thoughts and ideas for you to consider on helping you stick to your commitments to you and your freedom. Whenever you may struggle with something of your new habits and activities, ask 'how will I feel after I do this? how will I feel if I don't?'. For me, it's a matter of picking our pain. When the 'I really am not in the mood to do this' emotion crosses my mind (exercise, as an example), and it often does, I consider how I will feel by taking action versus not taking action. I know I will feel better following my plan, whether that be a feeling of accomplishment, happiness with myself for sticking to my plan, seeing the joy in another, or whatever. If I don't, am I really committed to it? When I miss an important part of any plan in life, the cloud hangs over me and I have to deal with the self-guilt or disappointment in myself all day. For me? The aggregated time I spend with those feelings is usually much longer in duration than whatever the very action item itself was. It's invariably a bigger self-imposed toll. Pick your pain on such days and stay focused to your 'why'. Some thoughts for your review:

- **Make a Commitment for 30 Days** to whatever aspects you are moving toward. Many say it takes 21 days for a new habit to become more permanent; others say 66; I think it simply takes as long as it takes. As a starting point, truly commit for 30 days with passion and a compelling 'why' and clearly defined benefits you are working towards. Will you commit for at least 30 days?

- **Triggers.** Triggers are events or happenings that cause an urge or an automatic action as a reaction, i.e. a habit in motion. They can be positive or negative, but are the potent initiators for much of what we do. Triggers help reinforce our habits to the point we do them unconsciously and routinely. As an example, let's say someone wants to begin each day in dedicated prayer (HIGHLY recommended to start your day with God). You may have a trigger of 'when I make that first cup of coffee (trigger), I will immediately begin my dedicated prayer time'. Maybe you feel you want to show more thanks to God daily. Perhaps every time you receive a text or email you say a brief prayer of thanks to God ('God, thank you for giving me a place to live, I am so grateful. Amen'; 'Lord, please open my eyes to grow my relationship with you'; 'God, please keep those who would discourage me from faith away from me or give me the ability to ignore their comments'; 'God thank for you today'). Prayers can be 100% yours, ones you borrow from others or a combination. Didn't make that green light when driving? Let red lights be a trigger. Caught in a long line at the checkout line in a store? Trigger. Sneeze? Trigger. Tie your shoes? Trigger. Turn on Tv? Trigger. Time to do laundry? Trigger. You get the point. Allow naturally occurring things or events in your everyday life now *begin to serve the purpose of serving you.* Beyond supporting a good new habit, it is also a way to reframe what have been simple negatives, like a red light, to being something positive, which is good for your health and mind.

Please take a few minutes and write down some trigger events you can use to serve you in creating good habits that stick and become part of who you are, in becoming what God made you to be. You can always add or delete some of course. Decide upon some however – it doesn't cost you anything, it's something you already see or do every day anyway, and it's a way to have life work for you. This is an easy one.

- **Automate to Make Automatic.** Allow technology to serve you in a positive way. In our connected and 'smart' world, we are inundated with information and alerts, most of which are unwanted and received involuntarily. Though technology is largely needed and has moved from a 'nice to have' to often times a 'have to have', reframe your uses for it. Allow it to help you more versus being a distraction, time drain or mind polluter.

  o **Calendar.** I have successfully used recurring calendar appointments, on my phone with reminder alerts, to help me. Whatever it is you are focusing on, consider putting appointments in your calendar so they pop up on your screen automatically and repetitively. The subject of course is whatever it is you are called to focus upon in your path. If you have no technology, then do it the old-fashioned way and write in on a calendar that you have displayed wherever you will see it each day.

- o **Newsletters and Emails.** Sign up for healthy, Christian based daily emails. These will naturally arrive in your inbox with whatever frequency you have chosen for whatever topic(s). In my experience, these are also really great. Even when I don't read a message's content, I know what it is and it automatically makes me think of it, even for a moment, which is great reinforcement in and of itself.

- o **Text Groups.** I know many prayer groups will send out text messages to their members, as do many online prayer sites. Consider signing up for some. How many really good, helpful and positive texts do any of us really receive now? Give it a shot – you can always unsubscribe.

- o **Screensavers.** I change my phone and laptop screen savers often to whatever area in which I am focused or in which I need reminders. Some I will simply create in a notes section, do a screen shot, and then save that as my screensaver; others I will save images from online. It doesn't much matter, but this is also a great reinforcement, which occurs however many times per day as you look at your phone or computer screen.

- o **Apps for Your Phone or Computer.** There are many, many choices for devotional apps, prayer of the day, scripture of the day, etc. There are plenty of free Bible apps available as well. Beyond great reinforcement, it's an almost effortless way to grow your knowledge, understanding and confidence.

o **Podcasts.** Same as point above. A quick share that literally just happened. As I write today including this section, it is on a Saturday and I've many hours into this, probably ten if I were to guess. Anyway, I stepped away as my neck and back are getting tight from being in front of my laptop. I took a break to step away into another room and read some emails as well as texts I had received. One happened to be from a prayer group of sorts – I literally have no recollection of signing up for this and receive very few messages from it. But today's text? A link to some great podcast messages. God wink.

o **Accountability Apps.** There are accountability apps for just about everything these days, such as fitness, finances, faith, exercise, diets, and many others. These can be quite helpful for those that commit to them and most are relatively simple to use. Some are higher in accountability in that you can assign others viewing rights to your entries and progress for a heightened degree of accountability and support. By the way, accountability isn't a bad word, it's a really good word, so reframe your view on it if needed. You hold companies or people accountable all the time, but perhaps never viewed it that way. You have utilities where you live? You call the company during an outage for repair. That's a simple example, but true. Accountability is a really, really good thing – see it as a way of how you are positively helping you.

- ○ **Social Media.** For those who are active with platforms like Twitter, Facebook, etc., follow and/or connect with people who post messages you find supportive. Delete, eliminate, unfollow and unfriend, any that are counter to your goals and realistically either toxicate your mind or simply are a waste of your time. And time certainly is precious...there is a reason God gives us expiration dates.

- **Visuals.** Display visuals of images or words that support and reinforce your goals. This could be notes you tape to your bathroom mirror, dashboard of your car, a place at work, your refrigerator, a note you place inside your shoes, anything. Place them where you know you will see them. Look around you and you will see how incredibly often this is done in the world around you, especially with marketing and business. There is a phrase in marketing which is 'top of mind is tip of the tongue' which simply means they want their message to readily always be in the front of our minds, as it drives brand awareness, which influences our choices and consumption. From a visual perspective, nearly all reading this without thinking can visualize the Golden Arches of McDonalds, the Apple icon, Mercedes Benz emblem, Red Cross signage, or a favorite sports team logo. Even if wording is removed, all would recognize the meaning of signs for bathrooms or stop signs. All evoke a reaction, consciously or unconsciously, usually due to repetition, exposure and attaching a meaning of sorts to them. These also tie into how triggers influence our thoughts and action. The point being what we know, think of or experience frequently or emotionally resides in the 'top of our mind' and is what comes out first in our speech in related scenarios of life. Fill in the blanks with what word or phrase comes to mind as fast as you can:

Peanut butter and _____ sandwich
Salt and _____
Up and _____
For richer or_____

You get it. If you will use visuals to be repetitive reminders and reinforcements, they can and will help you.

- **Communications.** There are many studies estimating how many daily messages we each send or receive daily via text, email, social media, television, and via apps. Naturally this depends on the person and usually the younger, the more prevalent. Years ago I was travelling for work and ordered food for pick up at the hotel restaurant. Another traveler had done the same and we briefly struck up a conversation, which was difficult, as he was practically glued frantically to his smart phone. I asked him in our brief encounter if he ever gives himself a break from his phone and he shared he receives over 600 work emails per day. Add on personal messaging to this, and who knows how many he received daily. It must've been like an imprisonment; and most likely a self-induced one. I believe we train others how we prefer to communicate. Some always respond nearly immediately to texts or messages of any kind, which creates an expectation for others to think that is the best way to reach us, therefore we end up getting a bunch and most of the time. Be aware of how often you are sending or receiving messages. Evaluate if something really needs to be replied to at all, if it needs to be replied to immediately, and if both parties would be better served with a real live voice communication instead (yes, there are many people who actually still do talk to each other). The 'connected' world is great in so many aspects, yet so drastically damaging too. Its public knowledge that software companies very actively research and develop apps to make the user community, you and me, addicted to them. Literally. My ask is you try to disconnect with electronic communications where you can. Take a break from the 'digital drug'. Much is unfortunately shared these days about tragic accidents due to 'distracted driving'. Usually the distraction is a cell phone. My youngest three children in particular have always been great with this – there is next to a zero chance they will accept a call or view or reply to a text when driving. I know this, so guess what? I don't generally call or text if I know they are driving. Beyond being a good habit, they set the expectation. In line with 'distracted driving', please also be respectful in not causing 'distracted devotion' to yourself or others. Shut off your phone during service, small groups, family time and You time! My longest friend in life and his wife began a practice a few years ago they have dubbed 'screen free Sundays' meaning all phones and tablets are all collected and put away for the entire day. I know many have done variants of this. Guess what happens to communications during these scree-free times? Meaningful communications occur. During a recent 21 day fast and prayer program at my church, as part of fasting, I decided to shut off my screens at 8:00 each night. I cannot begin to explain how relaxing that was, and continues to be. At a minimum, It's a remover of an often unrecognized or subliminal stressor. Try it. Disconnect for periods of time. How 'smart' are we really becoming from 'smart phones' anyway? So many dumb uses and dumb outcomes from smart phones. Cancel any automated emails, newsletters, advertising offers, and messages from sources you either don't want or are not good in nature. Remove the unnecessary clutter. Toss it out. And lastly, please consider what content you send or forward to others before doing so. Is the information helpful to them? Is it positive? Is it simply spreading news about someone else's plight, pain or embarrassment? Don't be a promoter of pain and negativity of any kind. Don't add to the recipients mental or electronic clutter. You are harming and working against yourself when doing so and are also absolutely harming others. None of this may have been even thought about in the past, nor been intentional. There was a recent story covered on main stream media including a short video. Like many other stories, it was quickly jumped upon by well-known nasty, negative news outlets, tweeted and retweeted, often by very famous and influential people, and of course everyday people too. And as very often is the case, time proved the story was false. When the whole video and story became released, the reality was quite different than the narrative that was spread with vile vigor. This automatic and enthusiastic sharing by probably millions, proved to not only be irresponsible and incorrect, it also proved to harm people, who did not deserve it, including mostly those involved who are in their teens. Even when the truth became known, the damage was already done. Many who saw this story and others like it, typically don't follow through a happening to the end, and only share what fills their need for rage. Don't be fueled by falsities to spew more sewage onto others. Think about those who do that, and the underlying reasons they do.

In sum, clean up your communications in what you can control with what you are receiving. Get rid of the crap, as it is like dust as mentioned earlier. Contemplate with good spirt what it is you feel you must or should share, and give yourself the gift of disconnecting for blocks of time daily, or at least weekly, from all things of the internet. It will be a really great gift to yourself and those you care about in your life.

- **Words**. Words, their use, and their implications are a massive subject in behavioral psychology, industry, education, religion, and probably most fields whether acknowledged or not. Experts are trained, and utilized, in areas such as military, marketing, court rooms and other avenues regarding what an individual says, writes or communicates. I think most people of course consider what words they use in any form, but not many have spent much time considering it more deeply, hence a few moments of your time on this subject. Why do so many people in positions of power have professional speech writers and communications directors? Because they need and want their message to be 'safe' and impactful for personal preservation and also to illicit a certain response by their recipients. They fully comprehend the impact words have. Some quick words from Proverbs (New Living Translation).

- o "Wise speech is rarer and more valuable than gold and rubies." Proverbs 20:15.
- o "Words satisfy the soul as food satisfies the stomach; the right words on a person's lips bring satisfaction." Proverbs 18:20.
- o "A person's words can be life-giving water; words of true wisdom are as refreshing as a bubbling brook." Proverbs 18:4.
- o "Gentle words bring life and health; a deceitful tongue crushes the spirit." Proverbs 15:4.
- o "Evil words destroy one's friends; wise discernment rescues the godly." Proverbs 11:9.
- o "Telling lies about others is as harmful as hitting them with an ax, wounding them with a sword, or shooting them with a sharp arrow." Proverbs 25:18.

There are a lot of words in the Bible, about words. I chose all the above from Proverbs, but of course you will find many examples elsewhere. As a side note, for any who have not read Proverbs, I'd encourage you to do so. Roughly 3,000 years ago it was written, and dang is it filled with wisdom as if it were composed just yesterday. Check it out if you never have.

A quote to consider from modern times about words by Former FBI Behavioral Analyst, professor and author, Dr. Jack Schafer: "Certain words reflect the behavioral characteristics of the person who spoke or wrote them. I labeled these words, Word Clues. Word Clues increase the probability of predicting the behavioral characteristics of people by analyzing the words they choose when they speak or write."

Thoughts affect our words, and our word choices affect our behaviors, plain and simple. They are very much creational in nature. We are told in Proverbs 18:21 that "death and life are in the power of the tongue: and they that love it shall eat the fruit thereof". Why did God tell us this?

Really give conscious consideration to your choices you use with yourself. Naturally there are many ways to phrase something, with very different mindsets being the result. As few brief simple examples:

- o 'I'm quitting smoking' versus 'I am choosing to become a non-smoker'. Or 'I'm no longer going to pay tobacco companies to make me sick'.

- o 'I have to go to church' versus 'I get to go to church' or 'God has given me a wonderful church congregation to give thanksgiving and receive love'

- o 'I have to deal with angry customers all day' to 'I get to solve my customers problems and delight them to make sure they have a positive experience'

There is a big difference between how these are phrased and the impact. If someone repeatedly says to themselves 'I am soooo fat/boring/dumb'; and that is the end of the statement and belief (whether fact or fiction), without any other changes, how will they see themselves in this regard in a month, year or decade? Probably not fit, interesting or smart. Words affect our psyche toward a given area, and again, that affects our actions. Words in part create outcomes, in the same way as thoughts do. I don't recall when, but used cars one day became 'certified-preowned'. I've lost my job three times due to position elimination and was about to for a 4th time, but I wasn't fired, I was 'downsized' and 'involuntarily separated'. Yes, there is a big difference in being fired for performance versus a position being eliminated, but don't the other phrases used sound so much better to those of us who've experienced it? What was once called a slum is now often referred to as an economically disadvantaged neighborhood. Homeless are often called displaced. There are tons of uses and examples, which are designed to be politically 'correct' or to desensitize the real word and condition, often times to push an agenda or stop one. We use them too.

The words we speak to others, as succinctly shared with us above in Proverbs is profound as well. Consider this simple example. I recently read about a Social Psychologist Ellen Langer of the power of words and The Copy Machine study she conducted. She was a professor at Harvard University and at the time and in 1977 conducted a study to see how words could change responses. A researcher would observe people at the library in line at the copy machine and would approach them to see if they could cut in line. They would ask three questions to varying people as follows:

Version one of question: "Excuse me, I have five pages. May I use the copy machine?".

Version two: "Excuse me, I have five pages. May I use the copy machine, because I am in a rush?'.

Version three: "Excuse me, I have five pages. May I use the copy machine, because I have to make copies?'.

The responses? Version one: 60% said yes; Version two, 94% said yes; and in version three, 93% percent said yes and let the researcher cut in line.

They concluded that we are more apt to do something for someone if we have a reason (real or fake). The simple example above illustrates how words make an impact of sorts. Be wise to the words you speak to others and self. Many studies have proven, which realistically we already know to some level even without reviewing them, that our word choices can and absolutely do create a significant difference in outcomes. Phrases about words have been around a long time such as 'it's not what you say, it's how you say it' (not always the case), and 'sticks and stones may break my bones but words will never hurt me' (ask someone who has been or is being verbally abused to great lengths if they agree with that). Be mindful of how you speak to yourself. Be alert to the words you say to or share in typed or written form. This is one reason I continue to encourage you to engage with very well trained and experienced church leaders, pastors, and mentors on topics that are very important to you in which you need guidance, versus taking my thoughts in the form of words and running with them. Please consider, perhaps in a new light, what you share with others that are negative in nature. When you receive something negative, off colored, gossipy, cruel, demeaning of someone, ask yourself if you really need to give those words on to others and spread harm? If you receive negative messages, will you give them more life by forwarding them on, or will you make the choice to let them end with you?

To the new who are learning faith, and to the tenured as well, don't ever be bashful about telling others you don't understand words or lessons. I'll go on a tangent for a moment. When in college, naturally there were prerequisites, as there are with virtually any kind of educational or training program. One was liberal arts in nature and I took three semesters of Russian language. I became conversationally fluent, but not much beyond that. The summer before my senior year, I went to Mexico for a program and was enrolled in learning Spanish, which I didn't know. Long story short, the instructors would exclusively speak in Spanish, thinking that students would learn faster this way through inundation. Perhaps that was a great technique for those students who already knew some Spanish. I knew zero, as did those in my tract of elementary Spanish students. From the first minute of each all-day class, my instructor never spoke a word of English. Literally, not a single word. I was completely lost day one; and day two, and into day three. Around mid-morning of day three, I couldn't take it anymore. When the teacher would ask a question in Spanish and students would try to answer, I'd blurt out something in Russian. This went on a few times. The instructor, puzzled as to what the heck I was saying, and assuredly I had blown her train of thought for the lessons she was trying to teach, finally broke down and addressed me in English. She said she couldn't understand what I was saying, to which I replied back something like, 'that is because I have been speaking to you in Russian and you don't know Russian. I don't know Spanish. So when all you speak is Spanish? I'm not understanding a thing you are teaching'. Long story longer, she changed the rules for our class, and began to interject English, which helped not only me, but most of the class. It also helped her accomplish her purpose and mission which was to have us learn her language. What's the take away for you here? Learn Russian; you never know when it might come in handy. In sincerity though, the message is If you don't understand something, simply tell that to whomever it is giving you instruction, as it not only helps you (and those you will help), but it also very much helps the one providing instruction.

No pun intended, but lots of words here in this section. Be mindful of your words and those used by others toward you. Words help you win.

- **Share.** Let others know what you are doing. It serves as positive reinforcement to your commitment. It lets others know so they may either support you, or change their behaviors toward and around you that they may not do otherwise. Ways to share? Verbally of course. The never-ending text/Instagram/snap whatever, etc. can also be your vehicle or among ways you share. Your actions of course are huge and are the most visible evidence of beliefs. Sharing with others anything you are doing or working on also adds a level of accountability and personal responsibility. I will share with many that I wrote this book. Actually, I will share with thousands that I have done so, many I know, many I don't and won't, but am connected with them via social media or in other ways.

This adds a really profound level of accountability for me as many will ask 'how's it going?'. This will help me in staying committed. Hopefully many more, either privately or verbally, will ask how they can grow too. A quick note on sharing what you learn: I have seen many across the years, hoard what they perceive to be good or insightful ideas or knowledge; and believe that they are the only ones that have it. Share what you know. From a knowledge perspective, the more you share the more you will know. Consider, as an example, if you decided to be well informed about a subject, more so than most anyone you likely encounter. When you share what you know, by default it will drive you to learn more. You will gain more knowledge by giving away (sharing) what you have. Make sense?

Two quick stories regarding sharing. I was in the back of my church a few weeks ago, and one of the pastors approached me and introduced himself. As part of the conversation, sharing faith came up and he made an excellent point, 'you can get to people that I can't, and I can get to people you can't'. He was saying I will naturally encounter and know people he will not and vice versa, and it takes all of us to move the needle, which is a very valid point. A second quick story. A few years ago, I was purchasing a car. After I did the test drive and was walking back in to do paperwork, etc., I brought a book to my sales person that was in the car, and told him someone must've left it in the car and I wanted to return it. As it turns out, it was no accident. The book was the Bible. The owners of the dealership, in all their locations, place a new bible in every vehicle they sell. I leave it in the passenger door console as its visible there, reminds me of what I just shared, and is a great conversation piece with any passengers that have or ever will sit in the passenger seat. Pretty cool way of sharing by the dealership owners, huh? It is also brave in today's times of protests, etc. but God has them covered with this great way of sharing with others.

Share in what manner works best for you; some are more introverted and perhaps electronic messaging works; others are more verbal. Do what works best for you, where you are, but share authentically and vulnerably, not by using someone else's words to look better or sound more official. An equally bigger component, is to share who you are with others, in times of need and when not. Brené Brown is a research professor, speaker, writer and author and has dedicated many years, decades actually, to studying courage, vulnerability, shame, and empathy. Regarding sharing about our true selves, consider this from an article she wrote:

"After spending the past ten years interviewing people about the truths of their lives—their strengths and struggles—I realized that courage is not something we have or don't have, it's something we practice. And, thankfully, something we can teach and model for our children. The root of the word courage is *cor*—the Latin word for heart. In one of its earliest forms, the word courage had a very different definition than it does today. Courage originally meant "To speak one's mind by telling all one's heart." Over time, this definition has changed, and, today, courage is more synonymous with being heroic. Heroics are important and we certainly need heroes, but I think we've lost touch with the idea that speaking honestly and openly about who we are, about what we're feeling, and about our experiences (good and bad) is the definition of courage. Heroics are often about putting our life on the line. Ordinary courage is about putting our vulnerability on the line. In today's world, that's pretty extraordinary."

Being courageous in the original sense of the word will help you and others greatly.

Simply said…. share. Share often and share authentically.

- **Others.** Purposely engage others. Attending church service is critically important, as is joining small groups/bible study/etc. I can attest first hand from years of my own experience as shared that 'doing it on my own', NEVER works as a long-term strategy. Additionally, it takes an inordinate amount of time, which can cause challenges on its own. Benefit from others, some of whom have decades of dedicated time, study and real-life experiences in whatever areas you are most needing coaching or counseling. Sharing is so important, it's a must. God himself said we are not meant to be alone, beginning with the first human He ever made, Adam. Why do you think He made Eve if being isolated was a good idea? Also consider Jesus. He chose 12 helpers, the Apostles, to be with him at times around the clock, every day. If Jesus took 12 helpers, do you think maybe that was a sign for us to follow? How many do you have helping you? If it's 0, that is a devastating, frustrating road I travelled, and also an easy one to remedy. Learn from my lessons-build up your helper team – you will find more eagerly willing to do so than you could possibly fathom.

- **Celebrate Failing.** You'll miss, you'll make mistakes, you'll wish you had some 'do overs', you may get frustrated. It's all OK and it's all going to happen for the rest of our lives. Know that. Accept this reality now regarding faith and freedom development as well. You will, however, fail or sin less in frequency and magnitude if you remain committed and focused. You'll fail better! There is a direct correlation between failures encountered and success. Failing means you are making progress toward something. Never compare making a mistake to not trying at all or having lack of ability to reach your goals. There are countless examples of famous and wildly successful people whose failures along the way enabled their success which are valuable to consider (research Abe Lincoln, Michael Jordan, and others). Consider Albert Einstein's words, which have been quoted in a couple differing versions in his making the light bulb, but basically he said, "I didn't fail 1,000 times. The lightbulb was an invention with 1,000 steps". Consider the Colonel Sanders example. Recognize most failures for what they are: very positive stepping stones to success and evidence of your effort! It is way better to fail at becoming the full you than truly fail by standing still and not enjoying change. Go fail baby! And fail often in this perspective!

- **Take care of yourself.** Value yourself well enough to research deeper into the three components of our design: spirit, soul and body. There are far too many really great books and resources on the importance of taking care of our physical selves for me to add much of anything to this, nor is this the place to do so. Briefly though, implement the basics we all know: get enough rest, try to eat and drink good stuff (love the food that loves you back is a phrase I recently heard), get some exercise, enjoy down time, and don't feed your mind with negative crap from outside input. Garbage in/garbage out is an often-used applicable expression in IT and database management. Control the controllables in your life and pray about those items outside your control that affect you in any pressing ways. Spend some time learning the difference between our spirt, soul and body, and then determine which you'll allow to be in charge.

A quick side-note. In a not too long-ago service, I don't recall exactly what the topic was, but it was related to valuing ourselves. My mind drifted a bit on this. My mind drifts on lots of things and frequently! Anyway, I have always loved cars, all types, and maybe this is why the thought came to me this way. Let's say you or I were given a $350,000 absolutely phenomenal, gorgeous, world-class, and completely unique car. Visualize this car in your mind (What color is it? Style? Smell the leather. Look at the control panels and dashboard. Imagine the comfort of the seats). The only small requirement is that we permanently keep it, and care for it. How would we treat it? I'm sure we would keep it immaculately clean inside and out, would read the owner's manual on all its functionality, meticulously maintain it, insure it, take special notice of where we parked it, perhaps we'd buy premium fuel, proudly show it and share it with others, display it at car shows, and maybe we'd even join some enthusiast clubs with others who had a similar make and model. All this for a car. We would not put vinegar in its gas tank, leave the windows down on purpose when it was raining, and drive it with flat tires. Not only would we not intentionally devalue it, we would dedicate time to learning more about it and its proper care. We of course are infinitely more important and valued than an automobile, but at times we all fall guilty of valuing and taking better care of things than we do our very selves or others.

Don't devalue or mistreat yourself (ignoring health, putting off prayer, choosing to associate with bad influences or influencers, participating in unhealthy activities, thoughts or actions, living in isolation, etc.). We wouldn't do this to the car above (or house, or job, or whatever), so why neglect ourselves, who are infinitely more valuable and important? You are most valued - take care of yourself - you deserve it as do all you encounter.

- **Pick Your Pace.** Decide what pace works specifically based on where you are, or learn your pace as you go. This applies to your time alone in prayer, reflection and study, church services, 1:1 sessions you may have with a new-found friend or mentor, time dedicated to groups, volunteer efforts and other areas as well. For some, going full bore might be their preferred and greatest option; others may want to take it more slowly and elevate their pace in time. A quick share in this regard. Many years ago, I visited a church and went to a session they had for prospective new members. It was quite good, loving, welcoming, and comfortable. I subsequently attended a service and I liked it. Shortly thereafter, I began receiving too many phone calls about joining groups, almost demanding in tone, or at least that is how I received it. I didn't go back. I am sure they had the best intentions, as they know unless people engage, they will fall off; however; it was way too much and way too fast for me, for where I was. It wasn't my pace then. If that all happened today, I would be on board. You'll figure out what works best for you, and again, enlist the counsel of others whose opinion and wisdom you would appreciate. Your pace should be in alignment with your passion, need, commitment and individual circumstances. It's YOUR pace, pick it or discover it.

- **Keep It Simple.** Don't fall into the trap of making a plan so exhaustingly long and complex that it cannot be accomplished. It's mentally defeating, frustrating and is destined to derail. Do make it challenging, a stretch; but don't make it unrealistic. I met recently with one of my church pastors as I have more time on my hands during a job search mode and I am investing it in more of my faith on a daily basis than I ever have. I sought his coaching and counsel on my plans with my development and his comment was that if I have the time, "you can never spend too much time with God". What a really good, simple, understandable piece of advice. Adjust your plans to what is happening in your life. Reframification has been on my mind lately. I view things differently than I have before, and that continues to happen, years ago until now and will also into the future. Regarding time, something we all loosely and perhaps unintentionally use as a self-limiting excuse, reframe how you see your available time, and preferences on its consumption. One small simple example: reading. Some will say they don't like to read and they don't have the time to do so. I'd ask you to evaluate how much time you spend per day reading text messages? Social media posts? For an average person with a smart phone, it's well over an hour per day, and is several hours for many. In reality, they read a ton every day, but haven't viewed it as such, as they do so in bite sized portions. 'I will read the Bible 15 minutes per day; I will find this time by spending 15 minutes less on my laptop or phone. I will read 15 minutes of the bible BEFORE I turn my phone on in the morning'. Simple, executable, easy to do. One closing point and share on keeping it simple relative to time and sanity. I can let my mind and efforts go down the proverbial rabbit hole on a given topic and I hope you go down many when viewing some of the scriptures and suggested action items. Many years back, however, I could do so to the point of frustration, trying to find an answer on something in any walk of life. I was at work one day when such an occasion arose. I finally asked a colleague and friend, Tom, a question about why something regarding a business matter was so. I'm paraphrasing, but the ensuing conversation was like this. He answered, "That's easy Matt. That's a blue whale". He most likely wanted, and definitely recognized, the dazed eyes and look of befuddlement in my non-response. "You know what a blue whale is Matt?" "Of course I do" was my reply. "It's the biggest mammal on earth, 100 feet long, many are 400,000 pounds. You won't find any larger living creature anywhere on all the earth. But for as big as they are, they can't swallow anything bigger than a large orange. You know why?'. To which I replied no and he responded,

"Because that's the way it is". I still laugh and think about that moment, but I clearly got his point. Some things just are and aren't meant for us to know an answer, or for which one doesn't accurately exist and probably is completely of inconsequential value anyway. I'll share with Tom I've included this. He doesn't know his sharing this saved me a lot of time and mind space over the years. Keep it simple - and don't let your mind take you off in time and efforts on blue whale type items!

- **Just Do It.** Don't vacillate or hesitate on taking actions on your plan. Just go to that church service, group meeting, event, your private morning prayer, whatever. When we delay, the 'bad us' can fool ourselves, and often does, and we slide back into self-deception and denial. Habits are an interesting and slippery slope at times. When we miss on something once, it becomes easier to do so again, and again, and again. Before we know it, whoosh! A good habit has gone (which will in fact be replaced, and typically by a bad one). Granted, there will be times when missing something is out of our control, but really love your pursuit of being a better you and having a better life enough that you don't cheat yourself. The ripples that occur are often amazing. Not long ago, I really was not all that overly excited to attend a Sunday church service, but I went anyway. At that service, the Pastor shared that a 21-day fast and prayer program was starting the next day. As I write this, unemployed seeking a new job, I certainly had the time to attend service and I committed to myself I would attend every morning service throughout the 21-day program. This meant I was getting up at or before

5:00 a.m. each morning, grabbing a coffee, getting ready and attending the service. This and an unexpected lunch invitation, led me to two men's groups formed by another church; I've met many great, interesting, excited and loving people; I've learned much which is immeasurably helpful, not to mention how much time and frustration it saved me on my own doing; and I've since joined a couple other new small groups. Why? From a human perspective, it was simply because I decided to get off my butt and get to church, the lunch, and try new things. I am the most immersed in faith from an others perspective and involvement in many groups and events than I ever have been at one time. I've simply decided to just do it, whatever 'it' is that is in alignment with my goals. Did that in part lead to my writing this book? Definitely. You think this book is helping me? Absolutely. Just do whatever is on your committed plan you have made for yourself at this juncture. Don't think – just do. This works in other walks of life as well of course. I'll go on a related tangent. I'd always wanted to skydive since my late teens. Over the years, occasionally the thought would surface. One day several months ago I was having a conversation with a dear friend. I don't recall why that topic came up, and it was only a few seconds, but I decided right then I was signing up to skydive, and I did so. The jump date was days away and I wouldn't allow myself to think of it, and it ended up cancelled due to weather and pushed back a couple more days. I again refused to think about it and was just going to do it. And I did. And was invigorated, and of course gratefully so that I landed safely from 13,500 feet. What do you think would have happened had I just kept thinking about it as I did periodically over the years?

What if I chose to really think about looking down from on high and read articles about chutes not opening? Shared with friends or family who would have said 'you are nuts' (which some did after)? I would have delayed taking action. Actually, I most likely wouldn't have done it, ever. Yes, of course there will be days you aren't in the mood to do some things or just aren't feeling the passion. Just do it anyway. Consider this perspective: someone who is routinely exercising generally would agree they have 'good' days and 'bad' days in this regard. On the days they are not in the mood to do so at all, but exercise anyway, regardless of their mood and mentality, they still reap the benefits of exercise, no? Lots of faith is like this as well. Faith isn't a feeling, though we are often blessed with great emotions as a result.

For good things, just do it. And what you are doing for yourself right now by reading this and taking actions, is a form of your 'just doing it'. It is for you, God, and others, and it is a very good thing, in fact it's a form of the very best thing you can be doing!

Chapter 14

Make the Messages Yours and Internalize

There is so much that we can learn. We can make becoming faithful as complicated, complex and time consuming as we desire. We can also keep it simple and digestible. What works for me with scriptures, concepts, or messages, is that I have to individualize them for myself. I've a 3-ring binder in which I keep notes, learning items, and also several slides of short phrases that resonate for me about a message. They either were thoughts that simply came to me as I pondered upon a subject, or are something I heard or read. In some cases, no one else would know what they mean, but I do. And it is one way how I learn and try to apply what God wants for me specifically or others. I do know, as should you, that these may change, be refined or be replaced as reminders as I continue to grow. Some items, just like any skill learned, eventually become a part of who we are. We become unconsciously competent, meaning it becomes so ingrained into our fabric, we no longer need to think about it, as its simply who we are. A few random shares of some of mine in no particular order from a reminder slide mentioned:

> ➤ Shame is from satan; Doubt is from the devil
> ➤ There are ripple effects from all we do or don't do: don't harm the innocent
> ➤ Do not let your yesterdays dominate the tomorrows of your life

- ➤ Firm and Finish the Foundation
- ➤ God knew everything I would do before He made me, but made me anyway
- ➤ Know AND show
- ➤ All people are = to all people
- ➤ Have conduct match creed
- ➤ He has entrusted me with me; and all whom I encounter
- ➤ Sin doesn't define us; a moment in time, a mistake. God forgives AND forgets…follow his lead with self and others
- ➤ Faith is now, forget past, don't worry about tomorrow
- ➤ Everyone has a specific path, each of which are equal in value and   importance. Stay in YOUR lane. God will write the story
- ➤ Unconditional Love – affection without limitation, under any circumstance and never changes
- ➤ The more I can be, the more I can become

I've included a screen shot of a couple of reminder slides I read each morning in the appendix if this is of interest to anyone as an idea. Again, it serves as reminders and reinforcements to me and are written in ways that resonate for me.

I'll expound on what some of them personally mean to me.

Know and Show. This quite simply is a reminder to me that I need to *know* God, and his teachings; and I need *show* up in life for others. This is a never-ending endeavor. According to the dictionary, some definitions of know include: to perceive directly; be cognizant or aware of a fact or a specific piece of information possess knowledge or information about; to have understanding of the character and nature of; to recognize as being the same as something previously known; to be acquainted or familiar with. As for me, I need to continue in learning about God's character, His word, His blessings, His teachings, His forgiveness, His love. I need to know it from a relationship perspective with Him. For me and how I am wired, I also need to know it intellectually if I am to help others, and myself. I need to continue to take actions to work on the relationship (prayer, study, attending service, showing love and forgiveness); I need to become competent in a given subject based on scripture if I am to help someone; and I need to show, meaning show up for someone, to be able to serve them. Know and Show reminds me of all that.

Everyone has a specific path, each of which are equal in value and importance. Stay in YOUR lane. God will write the story. This one is more apparent to anyone who reads it. This reminds me that every single one of us are created for specific purposes in whatever station of life He wants us to be in when we are able to discover it. Some are made for great riches through building wildly successful businesses; some are incredible teachers whose lessons and legacy will last for many years, or decades, or millenniums after they have left this earth; some are made to be great healers of others, either as medical professionals or through gifts of healing; and some are made to uniquely show up for someone else at an important moment. For me, this is a reminder to find mine, and don't compare mine to others. All of our roles are needed to support God's overall plan; if we were not, he wasted time making us as we'd be a mistake; and God quite literally does not make mistakes. This is a reminder I've internalized to focus to what God's purpose is for me is try to fulfill it the best that I can, knowing there is no finish line while I am here in this world. You have your lane too. Focus on yours and don't compare it to others. Yours is as important as anyone else's who has ever lived, is living or will live. Do you believe that? Do you? If not, come to believe it, because it is a very real reality. Talk to a pastor about it, pray about it, read about it in scripture, until such time you can internalize it and truly understand it, in your way.

Sin doesn't define us; a moment in time, a mistake. God forgives AND forgets...follow his lead with self and others.
Tied to shame, for not feeling 'good enough' or worthy enough to be part of God's plan, unconditional love, and forgiveness, is this reminder for me. I had a habit, for years, decades in fact of confessing the same sin or sins, over and over and over and over. I finally came to a point where I thought "I must sound like a broken record to Him". A couple revelations for me about sin and forgiveness. I wanted to know (see above) in both aspects (knowledge and relationship with God) about all the items mentioned. I'll limit this share however to sin/shame and forgiveness. Whatever we have done, or failed to do that is sin, is a moment in time, a singular failure at that moment. That isn't to say we often times continue to miss the mark and repeat some similar or same behaviors, but that is another subject. We, being influenced by satan or others influenced by him, fall into a trap of believing we are not good, we can't possibly be forgiven, and we often try to hide from God at such times. Just like Adam and Eve did. Those times are specifically when God desires to be closest with us. Let's be realistic: God knows everything about us. He knew everything we would be and do before He even made us. There is no hiding. But it is a common feeling. Here is one example of how I internalized

sin for me in a simple way. I played a lot of sports from a very early age, with football being my favorite. I first played football in the 4th grade. I am sure I made many mistakes my first year (and all). Did that mean I was a horrible player? Should I have walked off the practice field forever and never played again? Did the coach kick me off the team for making mistakes? Of course not. A mistake is a mistake; it doesn't define who I am. I will make more mistakes. I will sin again. The point is, don't fool yourself into believing you are what you did, what someone did to you, or what you did to someone. When we are truly sorry, repentant, and ask God to forgive us, He simply does and does so forever. He says so many times in the Bible. Not only does He forgive us, He always erases it from His memory. Yep, He told us that too in the Bible. Reflect on that: He erases it from His memory. Visualize a dry erase board after its been erased. He chooses to do so, every time. So those statements on my slide remind me of all of this, and remind me to follow God's lead. If He forgives me and forgets my sin, why wouldn't I? And since He forgives and forgets my sins, at the very least I can do so for others. If you struggle with believing God forgives and forgets, study and pray upon it and ask your pastor, leaders, or members of a group. Learn and internalize this one. It's almost so easy and undeserved that it doesn't 'feel right' until we really understand God's character in regard to this. And lastly, don't make a mistake I have made many times, by putting false boundaries on God. I realize I cannot fully comprehend everything God has done, is doing, and will do for us. I have made and consciously try to continue to make a decision to not limit or view God's love and abilities on a human level. When I think about 'how could I possibly be forgiven?', that's treating God as if He were merely human.

He most assuredly is not. Learn about His love and forgiveness – it is a critical foundation for growth in loving him, loving ourselves, loving others, and being effective in our world.

Firm and Finish the Foundation. During the 21 day Fast and Prayer program, our founding pastor at my church, touched upon generational curse type issues, briefly. That is a long subject for anyone who cares to pursue learning about it. What came to me to reflect upon was how I grew up, what were all my environments in life like, what was done or not done, etc. However, it also came to me to expand my view to include all peoples in all my experiences, not just family or friends. What happens to many when they are young as you know, can have life-long consequences, good or bad, depending on how the person has accepted, compartmentalized and processed them. As I reflected, a question arose to myself on 'how come people remember and refer to 'growing up' as an isolated block of time, as if time stopped once they 'grew up''? Meaning life and growing up really does not end; many of us just chose to think and behave that way. The thought dawned upon me that we are to continue to grow up, and create memories and experiences, for our children, our families, our friends, and our community. No one ever said it was supposed to stop. So in sum, Firm and Finish the Foundation, for me is trying to continue to create a legacy, and shape what that may be for all whom I encounter on an intimate level. If you were abused, neglected, felt unloved, or did so to others, is that where you will let it end? By end, meaning not progress any further and not only carry those emotions with you forever, but pass them along as well? Are you going to let what bad happened, or that you caused, impact everyone who meets you as you carry that burden with you? I hope if you have done so in your thinking and behaviors, you will consider it in a new light and continue your story, as it's not over yet. The same applies to any and all good memories and experiences in your past – continue to grow them and make more. Lastly, consider the new people you meet, and will meet, in setting a firm foundation. You have an opportunity to get it right, right from the get go, as that will be its own chapter of life, and you are creating it from the beginning.

In closing this chapter, please do make a conscious and consistent effort to make messages yours, in whatever ways they become part of you and that you can understand. They become yours then. Steal others messages that work for you (authors, leaders, teachers, etc. do this all the time – and it is wise to borrow from others what works for you). Do not however use a reminder phrase simply for show. Again, make messages personally yours. Doing so will help you grow, provide peace, bring you closer to God, allow you to love and serve others and become more of you.

Chapter 15

Readings and Reflections

Each of the next several pages will have some topics from most chapters and a few scriptures related to them; some scriptures for reading as references are given in each section, with the expectation that you look up scriptures where there are none provided and check off that you have done so!

Chapter 2	**Scripture Reading**	**Read it?**
Falling/Backsliding	Jeremiah 3:22	
Too much work	Colossians 3: 23-24	
Unqualified		
Shame	Isaiah 50:7	
Confusing	Proverbs 3:5	

Assignment/Reflection: What have been your struggles that have held you back from consistently pursuing and living a life of faith:

1- _____

2- _____

3- _____

4- _____

5- _____

6- _____

7- _____

Assignment/Reflection completed?   Y/N

Chapter 3	**Scripture Reading**	**Read it?**
Fear	John 14:27	
Shame		
Worthiness		
Isolation	Ecclesiastes 4:9-10	
Doubt		
Arrogance	1 Samuel 2:3	
Judging others	Luke 6:37-42	
Connect with others		
Commitment		
Conceit	1 Timothy 6:3-4	

Assignment/Reflection: List some of the areas above or additional which have been preventers for you:

1- _____

2- _____

3- _____

4- _____

5- _____

6- _____

7- _____

Assignment/Reflection completed?   Y/N

<u>Chapter 4</u>	<u>Scripture Reading</u>	<u>Read it?</u>
Laziness	Proverbs 10:4	
Procrastination		
Self-gratification		
Blame	James 1:13-15	
Peer pressure		
Exposure to bad influences		
satan deception		

Assignment/Reflection: List some of the areas above or additional which have been areas of deception for you, whether by choice or by not knowing better:

1- _____

2- _____

3- _____

4- _____

5- _____

6- _____

7- _____

Assignment/Reflection completed?   Y/N

Chapter 5	Scripture Reading	Read it?
Naysayers	Matthew 10:18	
Rebuke		
Encouragement		

Assignment/Reflection: List some of the ways you will remain strong when people are negative about your faith and choice to become fully you, so you are mindful in advance of them, let them shed off you and can use them as an opportunity to help others when they occur.

1- _____

2- _____

3- _____

4- _____

5- _____

6- _____

7- _____

Who might be some of your specific naysayers?

What might they say or do and how will you respond?

Assignment/Reflection completed?   Y/N

Chapter 6	**Scripture Reading**	**Read it?**
Scripture		
Inspired writing	2 Timothy 3:16	
Division/bickering		

Assignment/Reflection: List some of the areas from the chapter that you learned about the Bible or were led to view it in a new way.

1- _____

2- _____

3- _____

4- _____

5- _____

6- _____

7- _____

Assignment/Reflection completed?   Y/N

Chapter 7	Scripture Reading	Read it?
Persecution	Matthew 5:10	
Evil law creators	Isaiah 10:1	
satan's traps		
Lukewarm Christians		

Assignment/Reflection: List some of the areas from the chapter that you learned about the Bible's relevancy today or were led to view it in a new way.

1- _____
2- _____
3- _____
4- _____
5- _____
6- _____
7- _____

In what ways will you now stand up for God? Others?

Assignment/Reflection completed?   Y/N

Chapter 8	Scripture Reading	Read it?
Church		
Attending service	Matthew 18:20	
Leaders of church		

Assignment/Reflection: List some of the areas from the chapter that you learned about the church or were led to view it in a new way.

1- _____
2- _____
3- _____
4- _____
5- _____
6- _____
7- _____

Assignment/Reflection completed?   Y/N

Chapter 9	**Scripture Reading**	**Read it?**
Being saved	Romans 10:9	

Salvation

Who deserves it?

Assignment/Reflection: List some of the areas from the chapter that you learned about being saved or were led to view it in a new way.

1- _____

2- _____

3- _____

4- _____

5- _____

6- _____

7- _____

Assignment/Reflection completed?   Y/N

Chapter 10	Scripture Reading	Read it?
Learning faith	Proverbs 1:5	
Patience		
Aware of blessings		
Connect with others		
Serve others	Acts 20:35	

Assignment/Reflection: List some of the areas from the chapter that you learned about that you feel you need and will do to get started, started again, or to elevate the path you are on now.

1- _____

2- _____

3- _____

4- _____

5- _____

6- _____

7- _____

Assignment/Reflection completed?   Y/N

Chapter 11	Scripture Reading	Read it?
Spiritual gifts	1 Corinthians 12:4-11	
Honesty		
Calling		

Assignment/Reflection: List some of your spiritual gifts and characteristics that are "youamatic'.

1- _____

2- _____

3- _____

4- _____

5- _____

6- _____

7- _____

Assignment/Reflection completed?   Y/N

Chapter 12	Scripture Reading	Read it?

Purpose

Jeremiah 1:5

Trusting God

Answering your call

Assignment/Reflection: List purposes for which you feel you have been called.

1- _____
2- _____
3- _____
4- _____
5- _____
6- _____
7- _____

Assignment/Reflection completed?   Y/N

Chapter 13	**Scripture Reading**	**Read it?**
Putting God first	Matthew 6:33	
Staying consistent		
Physical health		

Assignment/Reflection: List some of the reinforcement activities you will do.

1- _____

2- _____

3- _____

4- _____

5- _____

6- _____

7- _____

Assignment/Reflection completed?   Y/N

Sample Study Exercises

Simple Sample Study One

What is Sin? John 3:4 describes sin as_____

What does sin cause as described in Romans 6:23 and James 1:15?

_____

_____

_____

Who sins as described in Romans 3:23?

_____

How many times are we to forgive sin as described in Matthew 18:22?

_____

What sins do you repeat over and over?

_____

Look up prayers about sin; commit to spend 20-30 minutes in quiet, private prayer focused exclusively to overcoming sin. Do more sessions of this. Make your prayer your own, and talk to God as your loving friend and father.

Simple Sample Study Two

What in your words is temptation?

_____

What happens when we give into any temptations? See John 1:13-15_____

_____

_____

How did Jesus respond to temptation in Matthew 4:1-11?

_____

How unique do you really think your temptations are? What does it say about this in 1 Corinthians 10:13?

_____

Look up prayers about temptation; commit to spend 20-30 minutes in quiet, private prayer focused to overcoming them. Do more sessions of this. Make your prayer your own, and talk to God as your loving friend and father.

The point to these simple samples is to show a means for some to further their faith: Consider an issue you have or want to know more about; read what scripture says about it; reflect and exclusively pray upon the area of need in a quiet space; have your prayer prepared you will say to God. Prayer should be personal, following what is in scripture, with a faith-based motive, and contain a sincere expectation in faith that God will answer.

Chapter 16

Now What?

That's it. That's all I've got to share at this point, so now what? Get to work!

Where are you regarding your commitment to making you the vest version of yourself? Check which closest fits you as you read this.

- ( ) 'I'm full bore baby! I'm all in and will pour myself into all I can!'

- ( ) 'I'm an 8 of 10 on commitment. I so want to devote myself and really know I will. I want to explore more discovery of 'how to' and what options are available'

- ( ) 'Eh? I dunno. I'm kinda' in my beginnings with all this stuff trying to figure out if it is all for me or not'

- ( ) 'I only read this because my significant other/spouse/parent/parole officer made me'

Wherever you feel you are on your commitment, know one thing and know it completely: ***you did not receive this book or read it by accident!*** While we may experience what we perceive to be randomocities in life, *this isn't one of them*. Please consider completing the suggested action items contained in this book.

What is the absolute worst that could happen? Is there any negative to doing so? You know the answer.

I'll provide a comprehensive summary of the actions suggested. They are:

- Read
- Reflect and plan
- Take action
- Measure progress and results
- Repeat

That's really all there is to it. Really take some time to determine your real and deep 'why's; establish the 'whats' that are your goals, thoroughly arm yourself for success through study and habits, and engage and connect with others.

God will take you the rest of the way if you do your simple parts.

Thank You!

I want to humbly and very sincerely thank you for spending this time with me. You, for whatever your reasons, are why the Holy Spirit nudged me to write this. It has been and is very rewarding to be chosen to do so. 'I am not qualified' never entered my mind relative to writing this content, as I followed the strong nudge to 'just do it', and this has been the most time-consuming nudge I've ever followed. I've been very passionate in constructing this, writing anywhere from 3:30 in the morning well into the late hours of the evening, without ever losing excitement or hitting a mental block. My hope again, is that my simple way of sharing my simple thoughts sparks you to discover real and needed change specific to where you are or leads you to people or resources that can. In the beginning, I stated '*I guarantee that when you have finished reading and get to the other side of this book you will have changed.*' I believe you have if you've completed all the suggested items, and perhaps picked up a couple new perspectives or ideas. Hopefully you got some attitude as well if needed! For those very new in their journey, this book and its contents are a small step, but an exciting one for you with a really cool, interesting, rewarding, edgy and varied path ahead. You'll see.

I would like to ask a really big favor of you. I'd like to know how I did for you with this book. **Please send me your feedback.** I won't have any way of knowing what kind of job I did for you without you telling me. Please share your suggestions, corrections, criticisms, thoughts, your stories, anything. I know this is a selfish act of sorts, but I truly and genuinely would like to know. I need to know your feedback if I am to get any better in my life, my growth and to become better for others. Please also share any personal revelations you have had that makes scripture understandable and 'real' in your life. If you got saved, that would be the big prize. All notes are so welcomed, needed, and appreciated. In doing so, please let me know if it is permissible that I share your thoughts anonymously either in a future publication or general posts I may share. **Please send any comments to Simplysaid7@yahoo.com.**

Thank you again for investing your time in reading this. Thank you as well in advance for any efforts or changes you make as a direct or indirect result of the contents in this book. As stated in the beginning, this is an investment by you, in you, for you that will spawn so many positive outcomes for you and for others. It's that giving paradox again, isn't it? Helping ourselves to help others, comes back to help us yet again. It's a never-ending blessed loop if we allow it to be. Never-ending.

Go kick some ass. You know what I mean. You've got this — you will succeed. I am praying and rooting for each and every one of you. You truly have greatness in you, every single one of you and you can discover it, grow it, morph it, and share it. May you find your joy, happiness and peace in discovering every one of your layers as you become more fully you. May you find your freedom and be a beacon of light for others. You can. I know it to be true, as God told us so.

Thanks again --- talk soon.

In Jesus's name,

Matt

<u>Appendix</u>

Sample of a Reminder Sheets

"Everything You Set Your Hand to, I desire to prosper"

Basic Instructions Before Leave Earth

The growth path NEVER ends

The more I can be, the more I can become

Everyone is = to everyone

One constant from beginning of time to infinity

Fix your eyes on what (who) lies before you.

Be fully present – 100% focus to the person.

God doesn't change; doesn't take back gifts and once are called, are always called forever. The cross before me, the world behind me, no turning back.

Don't let your yesterdays dominate your tomorrows

Never too tired to serve and there is always time available

Shame is of satan; Doubt is of the devil

He has entrusted me with me and all whom I encounter

Sin doesn't define us; its a moment in time, a mistake. God forgives AND forgets...follow his lead with self and others

Recipe: God's word, Holy Spirit and others

Faith sees the invisible, believes the unbelievable, and receives the impossible.

Ripple effects of all we do or don't do. Don't harm the innocent by actions or inaction

God is ALWAYS for you, in everything, even when we do not do that which we should do

Know and Show

Faith is not a feeling

Recognize and recall prior blessings

Be a listener AND doer

Have conduct match creed

God doesn't change how He sees us because of what we do or don't do.

Sin will take you farther than you want to go, keep you longer than you want to stay, and cost you more than you want to pay.

Claim God's power in healing, help, growth, struggles, blessings...they are abundant. View healing no differently than His

Israelites 40 years in the desert-God gave them what they asked for and they missed His blessings was about to give being able to forgive.

Generational and past – keep developing new memories and blessings: Firm and Finish The Foundation

Unconditional Love – affection without limitation, under any circumstance and never changes

Everyone has a specific path, each of which are equal in value and importance. Stay in YOUR lane. God will write the story.

For the world's sake, burn like a fire in me – light a flame in my soul for all the world to see

Love-Grace-Purity-Patience-Sacrifice-Selflessness-Commitment-Respect

---

"Everything You Set Your Hand to, I desire to prosper"

Faith is NOW, forget past, don't worry about tomorrow

Who does God say I am?

Comparison is the thief of joy

Tree of Life: Freedom, grace, eternal life, God is good and forgiving, not judgmental

Tree of Knowledge: our pursuit of Godliness, evil. Causes separation. Playing God. Bondage, the law, spiritual death, see God as only a Judge, we are condemned

Oaths to self don't work; often cause more of undesired; offer up all to God and seek guidance

The truth really does make you free

God has big and prosperous plans for you

Triune Essence   3-part design

Spirit – real me, conscience-must be redeemed
Soul-mind (thinks and reasons), will (makes choices) and emotions (believe, feel and remember)must be restored
Body-that must submit
Justification (saved) Sanctification (gradual)
Spirit dominated self provides protection from our enemy and strongholds, enables us to hear God's voice
That which receives the most attention = most influential and results

Who is in control?

Live On Purpose

It is for freedom Christ set us free

Emotions can lie; patience in prayer

Offenses: satan trap. Victims notice other's sins not their own; blame others, feel rejected, anger, resentment. Comes from pride. Jesus told us there would be offenses. Know it is of the devil, own all experiences, treat with love. No matter what happens, take responsibility

Love doe not seek its own; need to give and receive. 2 seas in holy land: Sea of Galilee receives and gives water out and has abundance of life; Dead Sea only receives water from other, no life, no plants or fish

God blesses those who refuse evil..these people will succeed in everything they do

Son relationship, not servant, Get to and want to, not Have to or obligated to mentality

Sheep follow shepherd completely, when they live with shepherd; know as they know they must for food, water, security, and life

Faith is root; discipleship is fruit

Exposure ⟶ Thoughts ⟶ Words ⟶ Actions ⟶ Habits ⟶ Endurance ⟶ Character ⟶ Destiny

I Am Sorry

I want to express my sincere sorrow to anyone whom I have caused any difficulties in life. Hopefully I have done so verbally already, but I want to take an extra step to reiterate this to those that I have harmed in any form or fashion. I also want to express it to any and all I may have forgotten about, or for those to whom I am unaware where one is due, as a result of insensitivity or situational blindness on my part.

I am sorry for any actions or lack thereof; words spoken or lack thereof; any communications, or lack thereof; deeds or lack thereof; any important events or moments I missed whether intentionally or unintentionally; any times I failed to provide help of any kind that you needed it where I missed; any times I didn't understand you needed words of encouragement or someone to talk to and I didn't show in that moment for you; and in general, for any strife, angst, worry, or concern I directly or indirectly caused or contributed to you whether willfully or unknown to me.

You Are Forgiven

I also want to share I have forgiven anyone who has caused me any harm, in any manner, intentionally or unintentionally; for any difficult unhealthy challenges caused to me, for which I was aware, and the many for which I was oblivious. Whether you have asked me for forgiveness or not, you have it. I forgive you. It is my choice.

Acknowledgments and Dedication

Thank you to God, for literally everything and never giving up on me.

To Mom and Dad, the most perfect parents I could ever wish for - the always and forever, exemplary examples and teachers for me of all things that matter. You have caused and created wonderful, loving ripple effects that will last for generations.

To Ashley, Taylor, Courtney, Alexis and Dominic. You have all blessed me with truly knowing what unconditional love really is. You have always been and always shall be my reason for this season of life. I love you all more than you could know. You surely have been my nudge in so many things that are good. May this book be of help and guidance especially to you, your children and children to come, and theirs. And yes, Santa is real.

I love you,

Dad (Primary)

About the Author

What do you want to know? You are welcome to email me with any questions, as I tend to be an open book, good or bad. As a summary however, I am a divorced, 51-year-old father of five and a grandfather. My career has been in sales, sales operations and sales leadership primarily in technology related fields. I've had my share of trials like everyone else: financial, career, friends, family, fitness, health, have had friends pass at young ages, and you know my faith journey fairly well. I will share that after I've been in the middle of the proverbial storm of bad events or circumstances, down the road a bit I am then able to see how they have all invariably led to blessings. All of them. Without fail, even the ones I failed to recognize. The blessings are there if we look back at such times with open hearts, clear eyes and minds. Those who know me best would share I have a zany and twisted sense of humor, am very competitive, passionate, and a bit crazy at times. Anything else you care to know, just ask.

The End!

Actually, The Beginning or Continuation....

Made in the USA
Columbia, SC
30 March 2019